CRASH

TEN DAYS IN OCTOBER...
WILL IT STRIKE AGAIN?

90-976

*We dedicate this book to our families,
who encouraged us through our
research and writing without crashing.*

AVNER ARBEL AND ALBERT E. KAFF

While a great deal of care has been taken to provide accurate and current information, the ideas, suggestions, general principles and conclusions presented in this book are subject to local, state and federal laws and regulations, court cases and any revisions of same. The reader is thus urged to consult legal counsel regarding any points of law—this publication should not be used as a substitute for competent legal advice.

Executive Editor: Kathleen A. Welton
Project Editor: Ellen Allen
Copy Editors: Maija Balagot, Wade Roberts
Interior Design: Edwin Harris
Cover Design: Anthony Russo

Published by Longman Financial Services Publishing
a division of Longman Financial Services Institute, Inc.

Composition by Point West Inc., Carol Stream, IL

Printed in the United States of America.
89 90 91 10 9 8 7 6 5 4 3 2 1

Library of Congress Cataloging-in-Publication Data

Arbel, Avner, 1935–
    Crash: Ten Days in October...Will It Strike Again? / Avner Arbel, Albert E. Kaff.
        p. cm.
    Includes index.
    ISBN 0-88462-843-4
    1. Stock Market Crash, 1987. 2. Stocks—Prices. I. Kaff, Albert E. II. Title.
HG4551.A67 1989
332.64'2—dc 19   88-32078
                                                              CIP

Contents

Preface

The stock market crash of 1987 was far more severe than many people realize. During those ten days in October more happened, and happened faster, than ever before. But some of it is not yet known to the general public. Definitely, the severity of the crisis has been widely ignored. The entire financial system in the United States came close to a complete meltdown. The crash represented a crisis within the operation of the nation's market mechanisms. It was not an economic crisis. With the exception of a few important indicators, including the national deficit and an unfavorable international trade balance, the general economy of the nation was in good shape when Wall Street shuddered under the greatest price decline in its 196-year history. Employment was high, inflation was low, exports growing. But there was speculative excess: Stocks were overpriced all over the world.

An article published in the *Harvard Business Review* (May/June 1988) by an author of this book and two colleagues has shown that investors' reactions during the crash were quite rational. It was a "smart crash."

Financial theories and the rationality of the investors did not collapse in October. The failure was in the market mechanism, the network that ties together the financial systems of all Western nations. It was a narrow escape from disaster.

The operations of stocks, futures, options and other financial markets are so highly technical that the warnings contained in the October crash are not easy to recognize. But once understood, these warnings suggest that immediate corrective actions are needed to prevent a future disaster that could cripple the interlocked economies of the West for years.

A number of significant financial and economic changes have taken place in recent years. The United States has lived through a relatively long period of prosperity. Large amounts of capital have accumulated. The stock market has become dominated by large institutional investors, while the role of the individual stockowner has diminished. The volume of trading on major stock exchanges has increased tremendously. Today a large portion of the market involves creative financial products that were unknown just a few years ago—products and strategies such as junk bonds, futures indexes, index arbitrage and portfolio insurance, to name just a few.

Trading is conducted through computers at speeds that until recently were beyond imagination. Electronic communications permit traders to execute transactions swiftly across financial markets within the United States, across financial products and across the oceans. Financial markets in North America, Europe, Asia and Australia are bound together in a network that can flash disaster from one continent to another. The traditional conservatism of financiers has given way to highly innovative investment strategies and, unfortunately, to greed. The market often exhibits great volatility unheard-of in previous years; prices swing suddenly and dangerously.

While the underlying financial system underwent radical and fundamental changes, some key elements of its trading mechanisms, controls and regulations, and intramarkets coordination, remain almost the same today as they were 50 years ago. To a large extent the mechanics have not altered much from New York's first securities trading post, established under an old buttonwood tree when George Washington was president.

While operating quite well under normal conditions, the financial system cannot cope with crisis situations and extreme changes in investor sentiment. This was frighteningly demonstrated in October 1987, but very few noticed.

The market system can be compared to a container designed to hold a certain liquid. Over the years the liquid increased in volume and became richer and heavier. Then it turned to acid, was heated and churned violently. But the same old container attempted to hold the liquid. Unless the container is improved, it will melt.

After the Crash of 1929, Congress took more than three years to introduce the first significant legislation designed to correct faults in the country's financial system. Today, we cannot wait three years. Markets and trading move too fast. A delay could melt the system.

The purpose of this book is to describe what happened in the ten critical days surrounding the stock market crash of October 1987, to show what went wrong during the crash and to highlight the critical problems we face and the disastrous consequences that may occur unless the market mechanisms, controls and regulations are redesigned.

This book contains a detailed factual description, often hour by hour, of what happened during the crisis. To this we have added fictional presentations of even worse events that did not quite happen during the 1987 crisis, but could occur now or in the future. The fictional sections are printed in italic to set them off from the factual accounts.

This book deals with critical issues that may affect all of us. We wanted it to have an impact by demonstrating the urgent need for change. A lot of technical reports have been written about the crash, but, as of now, they have been widely ignored.

We wrote this book for a general audience, but we hope that it also will interest financial professionals, government officials and legislators, who should take action to prevent the disastrous outcome of another crisis.

When there is even a small likelihood of a critical outcome (for instance, the meltdown of a nuclear reactor), measures should be taken to cope with the problem, to prevent it and to minimize the damage. In decision theory, they call this minimax. That is what this book is all about, and that is why we wrote it.

We avoided technical or academic language and we never dreamed of using footnotes. The message of this book is as serious as can be. But we tried to make it fun to read.

Avner Arbel
Albert E. Kaff

Cornell University
Ithaca, New York

1

October 1987: The Scene

WHO DOES BUSINESS ON WALL STREET?

Suddenly, Midland, a depressed oil town in western Texas, became the center of America. Across the nation, the plight of little Jessica McClure was played out on the television tube that makes the whole world a stage. For two days and a few hours, America watched while rescue workers drilled, dug, cursed and prayed in a frantic effort to reach the child who had fallen into a well so narrow that the walls choked off blood to one foot. Jessica, 19 months old, finally was pulled to the surface in a bundle slickened with grease, and there she was on millions of sets across the land for all of us to see.

Three days later the tube brought more unknown faces into our living rooms, this time from the New York Stock Exchange. On October 19, the Dow Jones Industrial Average plummeted by an astounding 508.32 points. Suddenly stockbrokers unknown in Texas or almost anyplace else in the nation were talking to us out of the screen, describing Black Monday: "It was a massacre." "It was a zoo." "It was a crapshoot." Thanks to the tube, all sorts of strangers can talk to us, but whether we better understand the world remains open to question.

The New York Stock Exchange came into existence in 1792, the third year of George Washington's first administration. Several businessmen who traded in securities decided to select a place and a regular time to meet to conduct their transactions.

They found an old buttonwood tree with wide branches that provided shade from the sun and some cover in case of rain. The tree grew on Wall Street, just a few blocks from the present location of the New York Stock Exchange. Under those branches, the 24 original members of the New York Exchange bought and sold government securities, which were issued to pay for the cost of the Revolutionary War, and shares in banks, insurance and canal companies. New York then was a city of about 40,000 people and occupied five square miles. In those days, just as today, people were unwilling to invest in securities unless the shares could be resold with ease. Thus, a marketplace was required for public transactions in stocks.

Today, the business of the New York Stock Exchange is much the same as it was in George Washington's time: auctioning securities. A building replaced the tree, thousands of companies issued securities and membership in the exchange grew to more than 1,300. In essence, the stock exchange simply is an association of brokers who serve as agents for people or organizations in buying or selling securities.

By 1987, an estimated 48 million Americans, about 20 percent of the population, directly owned at least one share of stock. But over the years, the nature of stock ownership has changed radically. Although they number in the millions, individual investors play a minor, almost negligible, role on Wall Street. The big players are large investment organizations. They own billions of dollars' worth of securities in corporate America. During the past 30 years, more and more of the trading on Wall Street has been initiated by big institutions: pension funds, insurance companies, investment organizations such as mutual funds, personal trust funds established by the wealthy and nonprofit endowments that support universities, research foundations and charities.

In the late 1970s, individual investors conducted only about 33 percent of stock exchange transactions. They occupied an even smaller part of the market in the 1980s. Their share of the trading had dropped to ten percent by 1983 and has remained about the same since then. Large financial institutions were doing about 90 percent of the buying and selling on Wall Street in the 1980s. Wall Street had become institutionalized. The influence of individual stockholders on the market and consequently on corporate operations has faded in the sunset. Individual stockholders played no part in the October debacle on Wall Street. But big investors almost ruined the entire Western financial system.

DEMOCRACY IN CAPITALISM

Stock represents a part ownership of a business. The management of a corporation rests with its board of directors and its executives. They issue periodic reports to their shareholders, often in the form of slick paper booklets designed by the best public-relations talent on Madison Avenue. In glowing terms, these reports describe corporate activities and earnings. A share of stock provides its owner with the right to vote in the company. Shareholders can speak their minds at corporate meetings, and often do, and they can cast ballots on proposals to management. Call it democracy in capitalism.

Louis Lowenstein, a former corporate lawyer and former chief executive of the $2-billion Supermarket General Corporation, now teaches business law at Columbia University. He contends that many investors today view stock simply as financial paper on which a handsome profit can be earned by buying or selling it. Oftentimes these investors are not concerned that stock represents ownership of a corporation that conducts research, develops new products or services, creates new marketing programs and provides employment to thousands of people who feed and shelter their families.

Lowenstein supports the old-fashioned virtues of investing in a corporation that you believe in. "If you buy on that basis, you will have made a judgment about that company and its businesses over the long term: what kind of products they make, who the management is, what kind of competition there is," he said in an interview with The New York Times. "No sensible investor would change his mind in a few days or a few weeks." But on Wall Street, stock dealers make judgments on corporate shares in seconds.

Today, Lowenstein says, stock changes hands too quickly. Shares are bought and sold for overnight trading profits rather than as carefully considered investments in the future of corporate America and its people. To support this view, Lowenstein says that only about 14 percent of the outstanding stocks listed on the New York Exchange were bought or sold in 1960. In those earlier years, most investors held on to their shares, casting a vote of confidence in the corporations that issued them. Some stocks, notably those of Ma Bell, were perceived to provide their owners with lifetime security. Stocks were purchased primarily as investments and not for trading. But in 1987, about 84 percent of stocks changed hands within one year. The big boys are trading securities as if they were baseball cards.

Lowenstein objects to short-term investment in a corporation. He wants to end it. He endorses a proposal that a 100 percent tax be collected on profits derived from selling stock that is owned for less than one year. Needless to say, on Wall Street he is a voice crying in the wilderness.

THE LITTLE GUY

Trading by institutions is a significant force in determining the market price of securities. Institutions buy or sell huge quantities of stocks in one transaction. In theory, the value of stock should reflect the current earnings and future prospects of a corporation. A share in any company should rise in price when that firm reports increased profits or announces a new product or restructures with a potential for increased future earnings. Indeed, that does happen. But oftentimes, regardless of a company's present performance, the future expectations of its operations can move its stock up or down and create a volatile market. Depending on how they see the future, institutions can drive the market up or down significantly by buying and selling vast quantities of securities in one day.

In 1971, long before the October 1987 crash, the Congress asked the Securities and Exchange Commission (SEC) to investigate the operation of financial markets and determine the impact of institutional trading on Wall Street. Even that long ago, the SEC was concerned that institutional trading was contributing to market volatility: Big price changes were occurring suddenly and veering sharply, and they appeared to be unrelated to a corporation's earnings or performance.

But conflicting views have been put forward. In a 1982 study, the Brookings Institute, a Washington think tank that has studied the American economy for years, gave a totally opposite analysis: "In terms of the stock market, there is little evidence to support the contention that price volatility increased because of speculative trading by institutions."

Baloney! Wait for the crash of October 1987.

Individual investors gradually have become indirect investors. For a number of years, more and more individuals have been putting their money into mutual funds managed by professionals, rather than buying individual shares. By the time of the October 1987 crash, bonds and stocks owned by investment companies, including mutual funds, stood at $1.2 trillion compared with $315 billion in October 1982. During the same period, the assets of mutual funds increased by three times to nearly $850 billion.

So individual investors maintained their place on Wall Street by proxy. But even if they never see a stock or mutual fund certificate, millions of Americans are protected by life, home and health insurance and are covered by pension plans, all of which invest heavily in stocks. Thus, except perhaps for the very poor, most Americans own a stake in the stock market, directly or indirectly. What happens on Wall Street reverberates on Main Street.

VIA COMPUTERS, BILLIONS OF DOLLARS

About the time that Jessica McClure dropped into the well, the Royal Swedish Academy of Sciences announced in Stockholm that J. Georg Bednorz and K. Alex Mueller of IBM's Zurich Research Laboratory in Switzerland would receive the Nobel Prize in physics for developing a ceramic oxide material that acts as a superconductor at the relatively warm temperature of 406 degrees below zero Fahrenheit.

When scientists learn how to shape the superconductive materials into circuit-board wiring, they will build efficient, relatively glitch-free computers that will leave today's models in the dust. But does the world need to hatch better and more accurate computers from the discoveries of Dr. Bednorz and Dr. Mueller? Yes, considering the computer failures that occurred during the crash.

Programmed to sell a stock or a stock index automatically and instantly when its price drops to a preset level, Wall Street computers click off as many as 60 transactions a second. *Click*. The computer just sold a bundle of securities, a transaction worth millions of dollars. *Click, click* and *click* again, 60 clicks a second. In minutes, billions of dollars in financial paper sold. Too fast, said some experts. It seemed that electronics, not business judgments, were running the marketplace. But surprisingly, in the midst of the crash, rationality and common sense took over to produce what some analysts called a smart crash. We will come back to this point later.

Until the crash of 1987, the term "program trading" was pretty much limited to the vocabularies of those who labored in the New York and Chicago financial districts and to professors of finance. But after Black Monday, program trading became almost as well known through the press and television as Star Wars—and probably just as misunderstood.

It's called program trading because it's conducted through computer programs. Simply put, program trading is an electronic tool that allows big investors, with the click of a keyboard, to execute a stock transaction involving millions of shares. As we will see later, program trading provides large institutions with a system to insure stock portfolios against losses. But did this insurance work when needed the most, when the market collapsed in a record crash? We shall see.

Program trading also offers investors who have a flair for numbers—and a lot of money—an opportunity to earn profits on small differences that develop between stock prices and related financial instruments such as futures indexes. A futures index forecasts the price of a group, or bundle, of stocks on a specific date in the future. Program trading became one of the scapegoats in assessing blame for the October crash on Wall Street. But we will show that computerized trading techniques may have been innocent, while portfolio insurance proved as useless as an airless spare tire.

THE GONG OF DEATH

In October, voodoo, those haunting rites of sorcery reaching out from Africa and the West Indies, seemed to be running the show in the little town of Florala, population 2,000, in Alabama near the Florida state line. The Honorable H. T. Mathis, 85, the white mayor of Florala, sprinkled cornstarch on the floor of city hall early one morning in September, suggesting that it was voodoo dust to drive out evil spirits. It seems that the mayor and the city council were feuding over a number of issues, including control of the police department. A few months earlier the council had promoted a black police officer with 14 years on the force to the chief's job. The day after city hall was voodoo-dusted, the new chief of police received an unsigned letter with doomful warnings from angered spirits. But the chief said voodoo wouldn't scare him away, and a city council member called the whole incident a joke that got out of hand.

Well, they weren't joking around at Columbia University when the administration decided that Asher B. Edelman went too far in designing a top grade for students in his class, "Corporate Raiding: The Art of War." Never mind the As. Edelman, a part-time teacher who worked full time as a corporate-takeover strategist, offered $100,000 to the student who could locate the best company for him to buy. Real-world teaching, said Edelman. An excessive way to mark a student's report card, said Business School Dean John C. Burton, who scrapped the prize.

Before October ended, Columbia University was not alone with problems. The stock market crash drained some of the glamour and a sizable number of jobs out of Wall Street. For several years, graduate schools of business were viewed by many students as passports to wealth. For some, it worked. They were able to convert their master's degrees in business administration (MBAs) into six-figure salaries on Wall Street. On university campuses, Black Monday sounded like the gong of death to MBA yuppies. Job opportunities were deflated or eliminated in the wake of Wall Street's severest wrenching since the days of George Washington. Whatever the future might hold, colleges across the country reported an almost universal decline in the number of students applying for admission to graduate schools of business. At the same time, law schools received more applications than ever before. Several deans suggested that perhaps Wall Street, where a number of illegal practices were being uncovered, needed lawyers more than MBAs.

CHOPSTICKS FOR JAPAN

Out in the real world, strange things were happening in foreign trade. In northern Minnesota, where hard times had fallen on the iron mines, Lakewood Forest Products Limited shipped out its first truckloads of chopsticks to Japan. What's that? The United States manufacturing wooden chopsticks for the automobile and electronic wizards who have driven us into trade deficits higher than Mount Fuji? That's right!

After every restaurant meal, Japanese throw their chopsticks out with the garbage, discarding about 130 million pairs of eating sticks a day. Japan is running out of trees for chopsticks and workers to make them. So Lakewood Products opened a $5-million plant to produce seven million pairs of chopsticks daily for sale in the Far East. At least in chopsticks, the United States surprisingly became more productive than Japan. With high-speed wood dryers and a computerized cutting system, the Minnesota plant can churn out chopsticks seven times faster than the centuries-old systems in Japan.

It was steel in reverse. During World War II, American bombers reduced Japanese steel plants to smoldering piles of scrap. The Japanese rebuilt their mills into highly computerized manufacturing systems, fine-tuned to the highest possible tolerances. Those old nineteenth-century mills in the United States were left gasping for breath. But the Minnesota chopsticks were too little and too late to cure the U.S. trade deficit that helped shake the daylights out of Wall Street.

When our story begins, Japan was selling in the United States each month about $5 billion more in merchandise than America was marketing in Japan—a surplus of $60 billion a year for the Land of the Rising Sun, also known as the Land of the Rising Yen.

No doubt about it: War makes strange bedmates. For World War II, Mitsubishi built the Zero, Japan's swift fighter plane, light in weight because it carried precious little armor to protect its pilot. The Zero could turn on a yen and dive like the devil, outflying and outmaneuvering the best from the United States Army Air Corps. But Japan lost the war. So what did the boys from Mitsubishi do? They set up an operating division to sell McDonald's hamburgers in Tokyo.

FOR CHINA, CAPITALISM AMONG THE COMMUNISTS

In October 1987, Alfred M. Landon, former governor of Kansas, died in his 100th year. In 1936, Landon suffered one of the worst presidential defeats in history. He won in only two states against Franklin Delano Roosevelt, commander in chief of the New Deal's social and economic battle against the Great Depression. Years later, a good-humored Landon described himself as "a lawyer who never had a case, an oilman who never made a million and a presidential candidate who carried only Maine and Vermont."

Also in October 1987, businesspeople, stockbrokers and tourists who fly across the oceans were given reason to pause. In London, the Royal Air Force Institute of Aviation Medicine published the results of a five-year reporting program on pilot performance. Pilots on long-distance flights complained of difficulties staying awake at the controls after being unable to sleep in noisy hotels between flights, or becoming complacent in cockpits with highly automated controls. Entire crews have fallen asleep with an aircraft in their hands, the report said.

After a 12-hour airport delay, one pilot wrote: "During the subsequent flight, because of the delay, all of us were extremely tired. During the cruise, we all fell asleep, only to be woken by the Mach [speed] warning bell. At the constant power setting, the aircraft had slowly accelerated, causing the bell to ring. I estimated we were all asleep for about 20 minutes."

In China, potentially the world's biggest market, capitalism was creeping in where communes once stood. One billion people form the most populous nation on earth, once described as a sleeping dragon. China: It's the Celestial Kingdom and the Middle Kingdom. The author of a 1930s book, *Oil for the Lamps of China*, pointed out that if you sold one can of oil to every Chinese once a year, you would become a multi-millionaire. Now, in October 1987, China's good earth was being offered up to entrepreneurship. Forget about Karl Marx, Vladimir Ilyich Ulyanov, otherwise known as Lenin, or Chairman Mao Tse-tung. New revolutionaries are in command in China, and they are talking about market economies to replace state planning. In Beijing, the government was developing a system to permit Chinese peasants to sell the rights to the land they farm, the same land once held in huge state-controlled communes. A lot of peasants could become minor capitalists. About 800 million Chinese live in rural areas, and in the decade of the 1980s, about 70 million peasants left their fields to work in new rural industries. Communist Party leader Zhao Ziyang said investment should be allowed to flow freely to the area of the country offering the lowest costs and greatest efficiency. Karl Marx never did believe that Communism would work in a nonindustrialized peasant economy.

They even reopened the Shanghai Stock Exchange, closed since the Communists won China's civil war in 1949. Shanghai established a modest market, a few tables placed in a room where transactions are carried out quietly. Missing in Shanghai is the split-second, rambunctious action of Wall Street, where traders often burn out before they reach 40. By mid-1988, only six stocks had been traded for the year in Shanghai, along with some state, city and corporate bonds.

It sounded like a dream. But the Communists who rule from Beijing's ancient Forbidden City promised the taipans of Hong Kong that they will be allowed to practice their freewheeling capitalism for 50 years after 1997. That's the year when Hong Kong Island and the neighboring Kowloon promontory—groaning under the weight of sleek skyscrapers, shops stocked from Fifth Avenue and the Champs Elysees, and banks that ship money by the tons in and out of the colony as easily as mailing a postcard—will return to Chinese rule for the first time since the British grabbed the territory in the Opium Wars of the nineteenth century.

China will be one nation with two systems, said its leaders, more and more of whom were showing up at official meetings in business suits rather than high-collar Mao jackets, the uniform of China's Red past.

A MONTH TO REMEMBER

October 1987: Without the stock market, it was not a particularly memorable month. President Oscar Arias Sanchez of Costa Rica won the Nobel Prize for his Central American peace efforts. "Now more than ever I am going to insist that a negotiated cease-fire in Nicaragua is indispensable if we are to achieve lasting peace in Central America," he said. The nomination of Robert Bork to the Supreme Court failed, and President Reagan's next choice for the court vacancy, Douglas H. Ginsburg, also was doomed.

Some 50,000 gay activists led by AIDS victims in wheelchairs marched past the White House carrying signs reading "Thank God I'm gay." Before he died, Leonard P. Matlovich, a gay-rights activist after his discharge from the U.S. Air Force, wrote the inscription for his tombstone: "A gay Vietnam veteran. When I was in the military they gave me a medal for killing two men—and a discharge for loving one."

The Soviets tested two missiles, firing them into the Pacific Ocean 500 miles north of Hawaii. Plainclothes police shot and killed presidential candidate Yves Volel in Haiti while he was delivering a speech in front of a police headquarters. Gary Hart, finally out of the Democratic presidential primaries following the publication of photographs showing Donna Rice sitting on his lap, told students at Brockport State College in New York: "There has been too much running down of the candidates who are remaining in the race today."

An overloaded boat sank in the West Indies; more than 40 sharks attacked; 13 bodies were found. The Minnesota Twins won the American League pennant with the worst record of any World Series team since 1973, and went on to victory over the St. Louis Cardinals. In a Lebanon prison, Terry Anderson, an Associated Press foreign correspondent who had written about Japan's economic boom during his years in Tokyo, observed his 40th birthday. He had been a hostage of Moslem radicals since 1985—longer than anyone else.

After Wall Street crashed in October 1929, the Great Depression followed, until economies were revived by industrial and work force mobilization for World War II. During ten days in 1987 that also happened to fall in October, American, European, Asian and Australian stock markets faced a crisis that almost wrecked the international financial system.

2

Wednesday, October 14

THE GREAT BOOM

Could anyone guess that Wall Street was driving straight toward the cliff? The view ahead looked peachy. The stock market had been booming since 1982, its longest bull market in 50 years. For five years, stock prices climbed steadily in 19 of the largest markets in the world, including the United States. The total value of stocks on all markets increased from $2,472 billion in 1980 to $5,995 billion in 1986. Throughout the world, it was a happy orgy.

Three markets dominated world stock trade. In billions of dollars, their growth during this bull market looked like this:

	1980	1986
United States	$1,391	$2,556
United Kingdom	190	440
Japan	357	1,746

Indeed business was booming. Not only did prices go up continuously, but so did the volume of transactions. The average number of shares traded daily on the New York Stock Exchange almost tripled, increasing from 65 million shares in 1982 to 180.6 million in 1987. But for many analysts, this trend was too good to last. They were not comfortable. They knew that the U.S. market was overvalued by a wide margin. Corporate earnings simply did not justify the high prices being paid for their stocks. A widely used measure to evaluate a stock is its price-earnings (P/E) ratio. To compute the ratio, divide the price of one share by the corporate net earnings per share. The earnings of each share is calculated by dividing the total number of corporate shares outstanding into the corporation's net earnings. Thus, the P/E ratio measures how much the market is willing to pay for each dollar of earnings. Typically, P/E ratios are high in a booming market, and at a time when companies are expected to perform well and the perceived risk is low.

Corporations do not distribute all their earnings to shareholders. They retain some profits to be used as they see fit, distributing the balance as dividends to stockholders. But the P/E ratio is the one fundamental measure used by investors to determine what a stock is worth. The higher a P/E ratio goes, the more a stock buyer must pay to receive a portion of the corporation's future earnings. Other things being equal, a low P/E ratio is a good bargain. Price-earnings ratios go up when investors are optimistic and are willing to pay a higher price for a corporation's current earnings and its potential future earnings. But investors can only guess what future earnings will be. It's like betting on a horse race.

Just before the October crash, the average P/E ratio on U.S. stocks was 23, its highest since World War II. Since 1945, P/E ratios in the United States had averaged 14.5. Thus, on average, buyers of American securities in the summer of 1987 were paying exceptionally high prices for stocks, prices not justified by the prevailing corporate earnings. Based on any historical measure or prudent security valuation, the market was overheated. Stocks were being sold for three times their book value, far above the postwar norm. And, due to the continuous rise in stock prices, dividend yields reached their lowest postwar level.

In Japan, the speculative mood was astronomically worse. The average price-earnings ratio in Tokyo had skyrocketed to 90 just before the market collapsed.

High stock prices also were fueled by takeover artists, big investors who were buying up shares in a corporation with the aim of gaining control of that business and bringing in their own people to run it, or selling part or all of it for a quick profit. Stocks of public companies are bought in the open market. Any person can offer a premium price for shares he or she wishes to purchase. In a takeover bid, the takeover shark attempts to purchase enough shares to gain a controlling interest in the corporation. A large number of takeover bids in recent weeks had been hostile, vigorously opposed by the existing executives and board members. To defend their position, corporate officers sometimes were forced to offer even higher prices for their stock, outbidding the takeover attempt, or to recruit the services of a third party (commonly called a White Knight) to do the same.

A new phenomenon had developed in Wall Street in 1987. It peaked just before the crash: evaluating stock by the *liquidation value* of a corporation, rather than the corporation's earning potential. The goal of some takeover sharks was to sell off a company's assets and make a fast profit. They looked for a company with undervalued stock, paying perhaps only 50 cents per dollar of the firm's assets value. When they bought enough undervalued stock to control the company, they could sell off sections or divisions of the organization at a price near their assets value, thus earning a large profit. Amazingly, only about two dozen major takeover operators were active in 1987. But they bought stocks heavily and set the tune. The rest of the market followed them, trying to guess the next takeover move in order to profit from any stock price change that might occur during or after the takeover. These takeover hitch-hikers were gambling on the market, not investing in it.

In 1987, a large pool of funds had been accumulated for takeover activities, funds capable of purchasing as much as $150 billion in corporate stocks. These funds were held by investment bankers, investment houses, insurance companies, pension funds, large corporations and wealthy individuals who were scouting the country in search of companies ripe to pluck.

Takeover specialists stalk their prey using other people's money. For this strategy, a new financial tool was developed, junk bonds, so named because they offer high yields but at high risks. Takeover artists borrow from the $150 billion pot and attempt to purchase sufficient stock to gain control of a corporation. This tactic is called a leveraged buyout (LBO). In a leveraged buyout, the earnings and assets of the target corporation are used to pay off the loan, a lot of it written in junk bonds. During 1987, up until the October crash, Wall Street speculators had earned profits of 60 percent or more while gaining control of corporations. By purchasing large blocks of stocks, takeover speculators forced the prices of those stocks to increase much higher than traditional levels. They had been using a wide range of LBO tactics in purchasing stock with loans secured by the very shares they were buying. In a leveraged buyout, borrowed funds are used to take over a corporation. The target company's assets not only serve as security for the loan, but the loan itself is repaid out of the cash flow of the acquired company. This was the game played by the big-money guys and the gambling hitchhikers, or leeches, as one analyst called them.

Big bucks are not required to play the game. At least in theory, anyone with $2,000 can start buying stock on margin, trading off shares for profits and using the profits to purchase more stock on a margin credit line, while putting only 25 percent down. And on and on it goes, a money-making machine based on the bigger-fool theory:

> Buy a stock and you'll make money as long as some other fool is willing to buy the stock from you at a higher price in order to sell it to an even bigger fool at an even higher price.

In addition to a $2,000 deposit (that's the minimum to start, but who would be satisfied with the minimum in this rewarding game?) followed by 25 percent down payments, playing the market with other people's money requires guts and financial skills. But hot-air balloons won't fly forever. During the week before the October crash and on Black Monday, takeover speculators had no choice but to sell extremely large amounts of securities from their bulging portfolios. When stock prices started collapsing in October, takeover speculators, the big ones and the leeches, sold off their shares with lightning speed. Margin calls (demands from lenders to put up more cash or securities as deposit) forced some takeover operators to sell stocks. Others were forced to sell to avoid disastrous losses against their credit lines. Takeover selling helped ignite Black Monday.

A few days before Black Monday, a potential kick was aimed at takeovers. On Capitol Hill, the House Ways and Means Committee recommended a tax package that would eliminate a number of tax breaks for corporate mergers and acquisitions. If passed, this legislation would have clamped a significant brake on leveraged corporate takeovers. The threat of losing tax advantages undoubtedly accelerated the selling on Wall Street that led to the crash. Facing greater tax costs, several takeover investors lost interest in their game, and sold the stock that they had acquired for a takeover. Other investors, seeing a takeover bid collapse before they could profit, also sold. After the October crash, this particular tax proposal was put aside.

Many practitioners on Wall Street knew that the bull market had increased stock prices to dangerously high levels. Yet, they wanted to enjoy the orgy as long as the party lasted. They expected that prices eventually would decline, and the market would adjust to its real value. But no one foresaw an instant collapse. Why rush, they thought. The exit door always will be open. The practitioners we talked with believed that average prices in the Dow Jones Index might fall by 150 points, certainly no more than 250 points. The decline would be gradual, they said, spread over a period of several months. Such a decline would be a normal market correction, one that traders had seen many times in the past. To predict a plunge of 508 points in one trading day would have been madness.

A NATION OF SHOPPERS

Wall Street is a high–pressure cooker, ideal for the young and ambitious. Traders not yet 30 years old were pushing their earnings into six figures, blithely believing that shrinking markets went out of style along with straw hats for men. The nation was prosperous. Help Wanted signs blossomed across the land. Unemployment had reached new lows. McDonald's was forced to hire senior citizens off the Social Security roles to bag hamburgers and shakes. More and more teenagers were finding better-paying jobs, or spending their summers with videos and cars purchased on easy credit or with American Express Gold Cards carried by newly affluent parents. Detroit finally got the word and put new oomph into the quality of its automobiles and the productivity of assembly lines. With the dollar deliberately devalued, America's labor costs became so attractive that the Japanese increased production in their U.S. plants and shipped Yankee-built Hondas back to Japan for sale.

The oil sheikhs were quarreling among themselves. That was good news every time we drove into a filling station. Energy prices were sane. The nation's biggest crisis involved Nicaragua and Iran. But a remarkable number of Americans couldn't locate either of those countries on a map. And when you got right down to it, a more immediate problem concerned traffic congestion created when a new shopping mall opened. America was a nation of shoppers, and malls sprouted like mushrooms in the 1980s.

"With credit cards and home-equity loans, we've become consumption-crazy," commented Paul M. O'Leary, a professor emeritus of economics at Cornell University. "We are overbalanced on consumption and underbalanced on savings."

Approaching his final year in the White House, the Great Communicator, President Reagan, continued to joke with the press. Whether he was seen as a great leader or not seemed not to matter. The engines were running smoothly, inflation was down, employment up and the world generally was at peace. The nightmare of Vietnam had emerged from its closet through a flurry of new books, movies and university seminars that drew no protestors. And most Americans expected that their income taxes would be lower come April 15, 1988.

LINING UP FOR GOLD MOUNTAIN

Japan was pouring money into the United States, buying up U.S. Treasury certificates (in other words, financing our national debt), skyscrapers, hotels and residential mansions—even golf courses. One estimate said that Japanese would spend more than $500 million investing in U.S. golf courses in 1988 alone. Britain and Western Europe were finding safe havens for their money in American corporations and banks. That well-known Australian shark, Rupert Murdoch, was sitting on top of a U.S. media empire, owning so many newspapers and television stations in the same market that federal law required him to shed some media properties. All the while, Murdoch's stunningly attractive wife, Anna Maria, was entertaining millions of Americans with the novels she spun off in her spare time.

Stock and commodity markets, banking systems and multinational corporations were weaving huge spider webs across national borders and the seven seas, creating, at least in the West, an economic *One World,* the title of Wendell Willkie's World War II book that contained a plea for postwar cooperation among all nations.

Companies worldwide were teaming up, taking advantage of expanding markets and split-second global communications to form megapartnerships that crossed national boundaries. One study said that about 12,000 American companies owned part of a foreign firm. European and American manufacturers were forging new relationships with each other. Caterpillar of the United States and Mitsubishi of Japan were joining to build giant earthmovers. Ford's compact Probe was designed in Detroit and engineered by Mazda in Hiroshima, a city rebuilt from its 1945 atomic destruction. Philips, the Dutch electronics firm, created a network of alliances to develop, manufacture and market optical storage discs with Du Pont as a major participant. Tata, an Indian conglomerate, and TRF of France teamed up in leather goods, Otis Elevator opened a joint venture in China with Tianjin Lifts, Alsthom of France and Bombardier of Canada joined hands to sell high-speed trains in North America, General Electric and Fujitsu of Japan entered into a $200-million robotics venture, and on and on it went in private cooperation toward an economic one-world.

Individual states of the United States were setting up trade offices in Japan and sending their governors to sign economic cooperation agreements with the world's newly industrialized nations, particularly in East Asia. Numerous governors were offering tax breaks, cheap land and other incentives for foreign industries to build plants in their states. State officials were peddling their home-grown products in Beijing, and inviting Belgian tourists to visit the Ozarks. So great were the anticipated stakes that statehouses from Albany to Juneau bypassed Washington and opened their own commercial diplomatic posts in foreign lands.

U.S. News & World Report quoted the chairman of Borg-Warner, James F. Bere: "Climbing costs for research, production and marketing as well as protectionist, environmental and labor requirements make going it alone in worldwide markets much harder for individual companies."

The United States looked so good that long lines formed each weekday morning on Roxas Boulevard and Garden Road— locations respectively of the United States Consulates in Manila and Hong Kong. Filipinos and Chinese were waiting their turns to apply for immigration visas to Gold Mountain, the name applied to America in the nineteenth century by impoverished Cantonese who came to this country to work in gold mines and build the railroads that spanned the West.

In 1987, Gold Mountain looked particularly attractive to Hong Kong Chinese. Margaret Thatcher and Deng Xiaoping had agreed that the capitalist colony on Asia's southern coast would be returned in 1997 to Communist China, the Middle Kingdom that had lost the territory to English opium merchants a century ago.

Every day, enormous amounts of money were chasing deals across borders and around the world. Unlike the old days, possession of money was not required to make money. Many avenues were open for using other people's money to get rich. Entrepreneurial projects were being put together with all sorts of imaginative and innovative debt: convertible loans (loans that convert later into equity positions), leveraged buyouts, bridge loans, zero-coupon securities (they sell at discount, draw no interest and mature at face value) and high-yield junk bonds. Glenn Yago, director of the Economic Research Bureau at the W. Averell Harriman School of Management and Policy at the State University of New York, estimated that high-yield financing (junk bonds) had raised more than $150 billion for growing companies in the United States since 1978. At any given moment in the United States, about $40 billion in new equity money was available for corporations to tap. You can translate that into $400 billion of total capital, because corporate takeovers commonly enhance an investment equity tenfold. Brother, don't spare a dime. Invest it. It will double overnight.

THE GATHERING CLOUDS

But like all coins, the dime had another side. You didn't need Nostradamus, the sixteenth-century soothsayer, or Nancy Reagan's astrologers to see that the view ahead was not 100 percent peachy. Among the storm signals in the autumn of 1987:

- Interest rates were climbing.
- Inflation was feared.
- The value of the dollar was declining continuously against most currencies.
- The bond market had collapsed.
- Corporate performances were being questioned.
- Erratic, volatile price changes were occurring on Wall Street.
- America's twin deficits, the national budget and international trade, were mounting. Americans were in debt to themselves and to the world.
- Concern was increasing that the nation lacked leadership.

For several weeks before the crisis, interest rates had been climbing significantly on all financial instruments: government bonds, corporate bonds and international bonds, particularly those issued in Japan and West Germany. Yields on actively traded 30-year U.S. Treasury bonds climbed to 9.94 percent, highest since December 2, 1985. But the largest companies in America, whose blue-chip securities make up the Dow Jones Industrial Average, were yielding only an average of three percent. Wall Street professionals call this relationship a high stock-bond yield gap. Bonds were the better buy. As the October crisis on Wall Street deepened, more and more investors sold stocks and parked their money in bonds.

A bond's yield is computed by dividing its coupon interest rate by the current price of the bond. An increase in bond yield always follows an increase in the economy's basic interest rate. When bond prices go down, their yields go up. High interest discourages business expansion, because it costs more to borrow funds, whether to purchase a house or to install a multimillion-dollar robot in a factory. Also, higher yields on bonds make stock investments less attractive.

In Japan, yields on ten-year government bonds rose above six percent, an almost unheard-of rate in the land of cherry blossoms because that country traditionally maintains low interest rates. For years, the effective cost of capital in Japan had been one to two percent. Similarly, West German bonds climbed to just below seven percent.

In the two years after 1985, the Western industrialized nations had been pushing down the price of the dollar in terms of other major trading currencies. For the United States, this looked good. In theory, a cheaper dollar would lower prices on American goods sold abroad, and thus increase our exports. The reverse would happen to imports: Higher price tags on foreign merchandise in the United States would lower their sales. The net result would be a reduction in the U.S. trade deficit. But the United States, West Germany and Japan never could agree on a proper level for the dollar. Given their clear conflicts of interest in world trade, the failure of these competing nations to achieve a consensus on currency exchanges is not surprising. Exchange rates are a key factor in determining whether a nation will profit in international commerce. Over a two-year period, the dollar declined between 30 and 50 percent against other major trading currencies.

In February 1987, the Group of Seven—Britain, France, West Germany, Italy, Canada, Japan and the United States—had reached what they believed was a unified approach on currencies. They agreed in Paris to lock exchange rates on the dollar into specified trading ranges. The finance ministers kept the agreed-to limits secret. An estimated $90 billion was spent by West Germany, Japan and the United States in attempting to stabilize the dollar after its rapid decline. But by mid-October, many financial analysts believed that the three governments had reached the limit of their ability and willingness to keep the dollar afloat. They would not expend more funds to support the dollar that was being bashed by America's trade and budget deficits. Whether the analysis was correct, this perception of an orphaned dollar led to further slides in its value.

In the three months before September, the world's major government bond markets suffered their own minicrash, a significant decline that surprisingly went widely unnoticed by the general public. In 1987's third quarter, bond prices throughout the world declined more than their income gained, and also more than their currencies increased in value. Thus, total returns from government bonds were negative during the July-through-September quarter, just before Black Monday.

On ten-year issues, the annualized return had dropped to these frightening levels: Japan, minus 9.97 percent; the United States, minus 5.56 percent; and West Germany, minus 5.16 percent.

For bonds, a five to ten-percent drop in one quarter is a disaster. On October 11, Larry Kreicher, a senior international bond analyst at Merrill Lynch, told a reporter for *The Wall Street Journal:* "There's a global confidence problem in the credit market."

Except for relatively mild statements such as the one made by Kreicher, early warning signals that the bond market had crashed attracted little attention. The alarm was drowned out by the frenzied greed of profit-making on the booming stock market.

While government bonds were staggering on three continents, trouble was brewing in the stocks of some of America's most highly respected corporations. But, again, nobody paid much attention.

International Business Machines Corporation, clearly Wall Street's premier issue, was generating about $54 billion in annual revenues. But IBM and other blue chips were battered in the week from October 5 to 9, when the Dow Jones Industrial Average lost nearly 159 points, six percent of its value, for a record one-week plunge. On Friday alone, the Dow fell 34.43 points. IBM dropped over four percent, a disastrous day for a stock highly favored by financial institutions.

THE POWER OF THE PRESS

The tea leaves were starting to form into a prediction. Beatrice E. Garcia, a writer for *The Wall Street Journal*, knew how to read those leaves perhaps better than any other person in the media. Writing on October 12, just one week before Black Monday, Garcia reported:

"The stock market's historic plunge last week once again raised fears that some computerized trading techniques, such as portfolio insurance, could deal another nasty blow to an already fragile market."

If October did anything, it made computerized trading—hardly a household word a few weeks earlier—almost as well known as credit cards. Amazingly, Garcia described a situation that some analysts would say, in hindsight, was precisely what happened a week later on Black Monday:

> "The stock market goes into a tailspin for a fundamental reason such as a plunge in the dollar, the Federal Reserve pushes up short-term rates, oil prices skyrocket. Portfolio insurers sell stock-index futures contracts to reduce their exposure to the equity market. Money managers who pattern their portfolios on the S&P 500 stock index decide to buy the now-cheaper stock-index futures contracts and sell the stocks that make up the index. Their selling further depresses stock prices, which causes the portfolios insurers to sell more futures and the cycle can keep repeating."

Just seven days before Black Monday, and with remarkable foresight, Garcia presented her forecast to readers of the column, titled "Abreast of the Market." This daily feature in *The Wall Street Journal* is one of the most widely read financial columns in the world. Financial executives in the Big Apple do most of their newspaper reading while commuting to their offices in lower Manhattan from the clipped lawns of suburbia. From Connecticut's Fairfield County, where the per capita income was the highest of any county in the United States, it takes packed Metro North trains about one hour to reach New York City's Grand Central Terminal. Lots of reading time.

Is it possible that newspaper reports such as the one written by Garcia helped to create a state of mind that led to October's big bust? Certainly traders were primed for a downward adjustment in the market. But warnings such as the one sounded by Beatrice Garcia could have tipped the market into a well-deserved reaction. Stock prices were highly overvalued, erratic and volatile. Market dips became more frequent, but were still followed by one rally after another. Wall Street seemed to have lost touch with reality. The market was displaying extreme nervousness and more volatility than at any time in recent memory. A 50-point drop in one day, almost unheard-of in earlier years, had become common. Brokers recalled with nostalgia the days when a five-point fluctuation made headlines.

Influential as it is, *The Wall Street Journal* could not have created the crash. But the newspaper diagnosed the disease accurately and timely. Amazingly, *The Wall Street Journal* had published an equally correct prediction just before the 1929 crash. On October 23, 1929, the newspaper ran an editorial titled "A Turn in the Tide," which said that the bull market had ended and a bear market had started. One week later, on October 29, 1929, the market plunged disastrously, and the Great Depression followed. The newspaper's 1929 prediction was based on a theory developed by Charles Henry Dow, who founded the Dow Jones Company and was editor of *The Wall Street Journal*. Dow died in 1902. But his Dow theory, as it is still called, was developed further by the newspaper's staff. Almost 58 years to the day, Beatrice Garcia followed in the master's steps by forecasting Black Monday.

A RED LIGHT FLASHES

From Tokyo, another red light flashed. Japanese investors who had been major buyers of U.S. Treasury certificates for several years, thus providing the cash to finance America's growing national debt, in September suddenly started selling more U.S. government issues than they purchased. Japanese sales outdistanced their buying by $1.5 billion. Why Japan reversed its position in funding the U.S. national debt is not clear. In most business situations, the Japanese are painstakingly diligent in studying every detail of an operation. Japanese have been criticized for lacking originality, for an inability to develop new concepts on a grand scale. But it is hard to fault the Japanese for the attention they pay to the minutest detail, whether it's wrapping a package in a department store or devising a sales strategy in an African nation. So, perhaps, with attention to every statistic in their data base, the Japanese detected the decline in the bond market that other investors largely overlooked.

To attract the Japanese back to government bonds, the United States would have to offer higher interest rates. But higher interest rates was precisely the wrong medicine for growth in the American or any other economy. The stock market hates higher interest rates. Japan's reversal in the U.S. bond market in the late summer of 1987 did not create a disaster. But imagine what could happen in a more extreme day:

Why Did the Japanese Bomb Pearl Harbor?

In Japan, strategies are developed by consensus. So, in a later year, it is not Mr. Abe alone, nor Mr. Yamamoto, nor Mr. Nakano, but all three of them and many more in Japan's bureaucratic government who, after careful deliberation, decide to drastically reduce Japan's holdings of U.S. Treasury securities. Instead, they invest Japan's vast piles of funds into European securities and new resort developments along the Riviera to profit from Western Europe's 1992 market integration. With the Japanese no longer bidding on Washington's Treasury notes, about one-third of the money used to finance the U.S. national debt is withdrawn. The U.S. financial system will eventually adjust, but picture the consequences over the short run: Social Security payments are cut. Bills from defense contractors go unpaid. Weapons systems rust.

Ironicially, for years Tokyo had resisted U.S. suggestions that it increase its own defense spending. Instead, Japan helped America escalate its own military budget by substantial financing of the U.S. national debt.

With Japan on the Riviera, Washington faces a crisis in seeking alternate sources of funds to cover its national debt. Japan's withdrawal from the Treasury-bond market forces cutbacks in many U.S. government operations. Should the FBI reduce its fight against crime and drugs? Should postal deliveries be cut to three a week, grants for medical research canceled, subsidies to farmers ended, taxes increased dramatically?

Drinking beer (imported from Japan) on the Riviera, where they are inspecting new investment properties, Mr. Abe, Mr. Yamamoto and Mr. Nakano agree that bombing Pearl Harbor way back in 1941 was stupid. Without firing a bullet, Japan achieved the economic domination it dreamed about in the 1930s.

MORE BAD MEDICINE

Another dose of bad medicine was spooned out on October 14, 1987, when the U.S. Commerce Department reported a $15.7 billion deficit in America's international merchandise trade during August. That deficit was below the July trade gap. But the August figure was 50 percent worse than had been predicted. Seconds after the Commerce Department announcement, the value of the dollar fell on foreign exchange markets, while the Japanese yen and the West German mark gained. Foreign confidence in America's ability to manage its economy weakened. So compelling are international trade figures in this era of intertwined national economies that they automatically trigger a multitude of reactions. The new trade statistics caused short-term interest rates to climb, bond prices to plunge and the Dow Jones Industrial Average to plummet by 95.46 points, its biggest one-day point loss in history, breaking a record decline set only eight days earlier. By any measure, this was a bad Wednesday.

Through October 14, each of the ten largest drops in the Dow Jones Average had occurred either in 1986 (two drops) or 1987 (eight drops). They were:

Date	Decline
October 14, 1987	95.46
October 6, 1987	91.55
September 11, 1986	86.61
July 7, 1986	61.87
March 30, 1987	57.39
May 15, 1987	52.97
September 1, 1987	51.98
April 13, 1987	51.71
April 22, 1987	51.13
September 15, 1987	46.46

But wait. The biggest drop ever is coming soon.

One week before Black Monday, Michael Quint wrote in *The New York Times:* "While the economy seems healthy, with no sharp rise in inflation and good prospects for continued growth, the financial markets are beset with doubts and worries."

Quint provided his readers with a quotation from Victor Chang, president of the V.C. Management Company, an investment-advisory firm in New York City. Said Chang: "The financial markets have the impression that leadership is lacking. Domestically they see no realistic plan to reduce the Federal budget deficit, and internationally they see a lack of the cooperation and coordination of economic policies we are supposed to have among major industrialized countries."

With an eye on the 1988 presidential campaign, Peter G. Peterson, the chairman of the Blackstone Group, an investment-banking firm, put the leadership issue succinctly and colorfully: "Talk about the budget deficit is a form of political AIDS, because if you mention it, you have to offer a solution." Peterson said the presidential candidates were avoiding the deficit as if it were indeed a plague with no known cure.

Political AIDS or not, the deficit in the U.S. national budget was infecting Wall Street operations. Since 1983, the United States had incurred a budget deficit in excess of $145 billion each year. The government predicted a lower deficit for the 1987 fiscal year. But "in mid-October Congress and the administration appeared to be making very little progress in achieving substantial additional reductions," the government's General Accounting Office said in a postcrash study. "This created uncertainty [in the stock market] about the government's future financing needs and the effect of those needs on the future course of interest rates."

The General Accounting Office, which conducts investigations requested by Congress, reported that, before the crash, the investing community feared that the "somewhat intractable U.S. merchandise trade deficit" was squeezing value out of the American dollar on the international exchange market. The falling dollar could detonate a series of economic explosions, including inflation at home. In October, market participants believed that some of these explosions already were starting, the General Accounting Office said. They gave this scenario:

- Foreign lenders were being discouraged from purchasing U.S. government bonds, because the expected dollar earnings would be worth less than they could obtain by investing at home or in other countries.
- The United States then would increase its interest rates to attract foreign investors back.
- If interest rates on bonds went up and thus offered higher yields than stocks, investors would find stocks a less-attractive investment.

- Paying higher interest on bonds, which represent debt, would touch off fears of another recession.

A NIGHT ABOARD THE *DOLLY MADISON*

On Wednesday night, the *Dolly Madison*, an excursion boat, sailed along New York City's East River on what its promoters called a psychic business cruise. About 120 young professionals from Wall Street, Madison Avenue and Seventh Avenue had paid $30 each to spend three hours between drinks listening to business forecasts from astrologers, fortune tellers and psychics. Just a few hours earlier, the Dow Jones Industrial Average had plunged 95.46 points, at that time the highest one-day drop in history.

A cable television clairvoyant known profesionally as Wendy, who is well publicized in New York, sat at a small table with a flickering hurricane lamp and looked into the future:

For 1988: Economic turbulence and financial conservatism.

For 1989: A Dow as low as 1,100.

The young executives groaned, not because they necessarily believed the dire forecasts, but to play along with a fun evening. One of the five women psychics aboard the cruise boat told an executive-search consultant that a lovely lady soon would enter his life. At that moment, the Statue of Liberty came into sight. "I hope that's not the lady you have in mind," he said.

Within a couple of weeks, meeting young women might become the least of his concerns. More than 16,000 employees on Wall Street would be losing their jobs.

A BUILDING IN TOKYO

Japan's Ministry of Finance, an awesomely powerful bureaucracy in a nation ruled by bureaucrats, occupies a long, squat and ugly gray building in the center of Tokyo, just a few blocks from the ancient stone walls that surround the Imperial Palace. Except during the Allied Occupation, the Finance Building, as it was called by American GIs, has been the office for generations of clerks, accountants, budget analysts, financial specialists, statisticians and bright graduates of the University of Tokyo, a principal training ground for Japanese leaders in government, business and finance.

After Japan's 1945 surrender, the Finance Building was expropri-
ated by General Douglas A. MacArthur's military occupation headquarters and used as a billet for American enlisted men until the
early 1950s. Picture, if you can, GIs standing in chow lines, sleeping
on iron cots and shouting obscenities in showers installed in the
chambers of finance that served the Empire of Japan when its borders extended from the Siberian border south to the subtropics of
Taiwan.

Restored to glory, the Finance Building today serves as the cock-
pit of an economy so huge that, in comparison, Japan's World War
II scheme for a Greater East Asia Co-Prosperity Sphere looks like a
mom-and-pop store. Today's denizens of the Finance Building wield
power that reaches around the world—to the City in London, to the
Bourse in Paris, to Wall Street in Manhattan and to the sheikhs in
Riyadh.

On Wednesday, the bureaucrats in the Finance Building and
traders at the Tokyo Stock Exchange were watching the developing
trouble in New York. Given Japan's immense buying and selling
power, Tokyo's next move may be critical for Wall Street.

3

Thursday, October 15

THREE-LEGGED UNDERWEAR

Soichiro Honda, 82, has been known to wear pink suits. He rejects the ancient Japanese tradition that all people should fit into a common mold. "Pound down the nail that sticks up," says a Japanese proverb. But not Honda. The iconoclastic founder of Honda Motor Company built a motorcycle and automobile empire in Japan with innovative research, manufacturing and marketing strategies that cast him outside the pale of that nation's traditional old-line industrial and business conglomorates, the *zaibatsu*.

The literal translation of *zaibatsu* is "property family." Founded in earlier centuries and once family-owned, *zaibatsu* organizations include the giant Mitsubishi and Mitsui groups that trade in everything from noodles to supertankers. Bureaucratic and conservative, *zaibatsu* companies earn fantastic profits through close coordination between their banking, insurance, manufacturing and marketing branches. Since World War II, a number of Japanese firms have developed outside the *zaibatsu* circle into world prominence, including such famous brand names as Sony and Honda.

Soichiro Honda devised some maverick approaches to develop a spirit of entrepreneurship among his people. So it comes as no surprise to learn that one of Honda's workers built a bathtub to fit in the rear of an automobile, and another employee designed underwear for three legs.

Since 1970, in a mixture of fun and entrepreneurship, Honda Motor Company has encouraged its workers to use company equipment and supplies to build whatever outlandish devices their minds might conceive. The company's goal is not to discover new products (the car bathtub splashed water into the front seat while being driven), but rather to inspire its factory hands toward bold and inventive thinking.

The autumn 1987 display of worker-built contraptions in Hondaland, the company's amusement park in Suzuka, Japan, seemed tailored for a sales pitch: a pillow with a built-in wake-up alarm, a mechanized sled that climbs back up a hill after a slide, a toothbrush with built-in toothpaste and plants that dance to mambo music. The underwear with three leg holes? The inventor said the garment could be worn for six days without laundering by rotating it one-third cycle each day for three days and then turning it inside out and repeating the process for three more days.

10 A.M.: TUMBLING BONDS

Perhaps the New York Stock Exchange could use an extra leg. When markets opened this morning, they looked pretty shaky. Short-term and long-term interest rates were climbing. Bond prices had just set a new low for the year, bond yields were dangerously high and the stock market was pointed downwards.

Writing in *The New York Times*, Michael Quint reported: "The fear in the credit markets is that the Federal Reserve will soon be forced to push short-term interest rates higher to prevent continued declines in the dollar's value. If the dollar is allowed to fall sharply . . . it would lead to more foreign selling of Treasury bonds and higher inflation as prices of imports rise."

The headline on his report read: "Rates Up in Wild Trading."

Thomas A. Lawler, a vice president and economist at the Federal National Mortgage Association, said: "The increase of nearly three percentage points in bond yields since March is more than we expected, and there are signs that it is beginning to have an economic impact." Bond yield increases when the bond price decreases.

When the market opened this morning, prices on Treasury bonds started to tumble. By 10 A.M., a bellwether Treasury issue had dropped more than 1⅝ points to the day's low of about 86 points, pushing its yield above the critical ten percent bench mark to 10.36 points. But bond prices later gained after the Federal Reserve temporarily bought securities for its own account an hour earlier than normal. Allan Leslie, a vice president at Discount Corporation, viewed the Fed's move as its way to calm the financial market. But evidently the Fed's intervention in the market was not enough.

10:48 A.M.: AN ASSAULT ON INTEREST RATES

The morning started with discouraging news from the nation's retailers, who perhaps wished they could display an alarm-clock pillow or dancing flowers to reverse declining sales.

The Commerce Department said that retail sales in September fell $500 million from August, a decline that economists interpreted as a trend that would continue because debt-burdened consumers were cutting back on spending. Retail sales of $128.8 billion-worth of merchandise in September represented a fall of four-tenths of one percent from the previous month. Retail figures were strong in July and August. But when September results were posted, Undersecretary of Commerce Robert Ortner told news reporters: "I think the consumer sector of the economy is going to settle into a sluggish pattern at best."

Depressed retail activity resulted in large measure from a sharp decline in auto sales, a major barometer in measuring the health of the U.S. economy. About three percent of America's gross national product is wrapped up in the automobile industry. Car sales dropped 1.4 percent in September after a 5.7 percent increase in August. October was worse. On September 30, General Motors Corporation, Ford Motor Company and Chrysler Corporation ended their sales-incentive programs designed to clear remaining 1987 models out of showrooms.

The end to cash rebates and low-interest car loans brought swift reaction. On October 14, Detroit reported that sales of automobiles manufactured in North America had braked sharply and plunged 39 percent in the first ten days of the month compared with a year earlier: declining from 247,623 cars sold in the first part of October 1986 to 151,043 in October 1987. To save the market, analysts said that car dealers would be forced again to offer discounts and low-cost financing. "If they don't, they'll be hip-deep in cars by December," *The Wall Street Journal* reported from John Qualls, an economist with Monsanto Corporation, a supplier to the auto industry.

Traders on Wall Street react to news and information faster than rain dampens the dust on a parched corn field in Iowa. Stock prices plunge moments after a military attack in the Persian Gulf. Pessimistic economic statistics can blow Wall Streeters off their feet regardless of what the figures measure: national debt, trade deficit, unemployment, housing starts, grain and oilseed futures, cocoa, coffee, sugar, cotton, metals, monetary exchange rates, the price of pork bellies in Chicago or retail sales from Hoboken to Honolulu.

Thus, depressed auto and other retail sales did not bode well when the market opened today. Other factors that could dampen the economy developed during the day. Chemical Bank of New York raised its prime lending rate by one-half of a percentage point to 9¾ percent, its highest level in more than two years. Chemical, owned by the nation's fourth-largest bank holding company, increased the cost of its money just one week after most banks had raised the prime one-half point to 9¼ percent. An increase in prime interest rates particularly hurt small-size and medium-size businesses, the foundation of the nation's economy and employment. Large corporations normally can obtain alternate financing at interest rates below prime. Also, home-equity loans used by more and more Americans to finance their styles of living—sometimes at a higher level than prudence dictates—are based on the prime rate.

But, above all, higher interest rates warn of more trouble to come: a higher cost of borrowing, less consumer spending, lower economic growth, higher production costs, more bankruptcies, and higher inflation. A high interest rate is the stock market's worst enemy.

Along with twin deficits in the national budget and foreign trade, fears of higher interest rates were reducing stock and bond prices. This morning *The New York Times* reported that rumors were sweeping the market that the discount rate might be increased again. This is the rate the Fed charges on its loans to banks. In turn, banks cover the increase by raising interest on their loans to businesses and consumers. In Washington this morning, Treasury Secretary James A. Baker III and Beryl W. Sprinkel, President Reagan's chief economist, met with reporters in an effort to calm economic worries.

Baker painted a pleasant picture of the nation: nearly five years of economic growth, low unemployment, relatively low interest rates and progress in reducing the national budget deficit. But he admitted that the economy remained troubled with a large international trade deficit, falling stock prices and interest rates that admittedly were increasing. But he said he couldn't do much when banks increase their prime rates as Chemical had just done. "We don't get into the business of arm-twisting the banks," he told reporters.

At 10:48 A.M., earlier in the day than usual, the Federal Reserve injected funds into the banking system in a move that analysts interpreted as a signal that the Fed would not push up short-term interest rates at this time.

12:30 P.M.: PENSION FUNDS SELL

Yesterday an Iranian missile, probably a Silkworm made in China, hit the starboard side of the American-owned oil tanker *Sungari* while it lay at anchor off Al Ahmadi, Kuwait's main oil-loading terminal, setting the tanker afire. Wall Street traders, sensitive to any event that might upset the world, could breathe easily this time. The Pentagon ruled out a response. The vessel was not in international waters and, although American-owned, it was flying the Liberian flag. A note for international harmony was struck in the United Nations. The Soviet Union announced that it was paying all its outstanding debts to the world organization including $197 million for U.N. peace-keeping operations long opposed by Moscow.

But harmony did not prevail on Wall Street. The fall in bond prices pushed their yields even higher, encouraging some investors to shift from lower-yielding stocks to bonds. In Annapolis, Maryland, the state employees' pension plan announced that it had sold more than $2.3 billion-worth of common stock and purchased $4 billion in bonds. Bennett Shaver, executive director of the Maryland plan, said the pension fund earned substantial gains on its stock portfolio and took advantage of ten-percent yields on high-quality bonds. Managers of state pension funds in New Jersey ($20 billion) and Colorado ($7.5 billion) also said they had reduced or were planning to reduce the portion of stocks in their portfolios, and to replace the equities with other investments.

To people who understand the signals in financial markets, movement out of stocks into other investments is bad news. As bad as it was in 1987, imagine what could happen at some future date if even more stocks were drained from pension funds.

Up Goes the Dinner Check

No market can operate without public trust.

Once again, in a future year, stock prices are falling. Pensioners worry about the state of affairs on Wall Street. Printers collaborate with traders and slip them advance copies of financial magazines containing stock recommendations. Reporters pocket commissions by tipping off traders on what they are going to write in their newspapers. Many years ago, a foreign correspondent in a tropical Asian country augmented his modest journalist salary by recklessly manipulating a rubber market with his news dispatches.

Pensioners are alarmed by market activities they fear will erode their lifeline: the stocks supporting their pensions. Insider trading. Leveraged buyouts. Billion-dollar mergers. Young MBA graduates masterminding million-dollar deals. Stock exchange traders ignoring corporate performances, while capitalizing for themselves on thin spreads between stock prices and future indexes. To pensioners, the market sounds more like gambling than investing. They write letters of concern to pensions managers.

Conservative by nature, committed to the good men and women who had retired after lifetimes of loyal service, pension managers also question the market's integrity and security. So they sell stocks by the billions of dollars, investing instead in bonds, prime real estate and certificates of deposit.

The stock market plunges so low that many people fear that stock certificates will soon become as worthless as Chinese money in 1949. In that year, just before Generalissimo Chiang Kai-shek lost his last battle to the Chinese Communists, the price of dinner in a Shanghai restaurant actually increased before the last course was served.

3 P.M.: A FAST TRACK

At 12:30 P.M. today, the Dow Jones had advanced 15.50 points, but a rout was ahead.

With storm signals flying over Wall Street, a metal sign was posted at the block-trading desk of Shearson Lehman Hutton. The sign displayed an arrow and read: "To the Lifeboats."

Already in the past month, nearly 1,100 people have lost their jobs on Wall Street as the market turned down. Some of them earned six-figure salaries. Young MBA graduates had become overpaid yuppies with dreams of riding forever on the up escalator, the roaring bull market. But by October, the bulls were vanquished. Since its August 25 peak, the Dow Jones Industrial Average had dropped 13.5 percent. "We're going to have to run our firms like regular businesses instead of with the bull market at our backs," said Max C. Chapman, Jr., president of Kidder, Peabody and Company. His firm was cutting 100 people from its 280-person staff in municipal bonds.

In Boston on September 8, James Segel joined Salomon Brothers as vice president for public finance after serving as a Massachusetts state legislator and a lobbyist. Five weeks later, Salomon abandoned its public finance business and Segel was out of a job. "They told me they would put me on a fast track," he said, "but this is a little faster than I expected."

Yesterday, the Dow Jones fell by a record 95.46 points. Institutional and individual investors were growing increasingly anxious over the future of the market. Capital was moving from stocks into bonds. The Dow climbed through the morning and then fell, then inched up slightly, fell again and then started a recovery. Such fluctuations were evil signals. Watching prices flash past on the board, Alex Thiotos, a limousine driver from Queens, New York, said, "The market just seems to take one step forward, three steps back. I don't like it."

At 3 P.M., the Dow was fractionally ahead of its opening.

4 P.M.: BAD NEWS ON TRADE

In Japan they were smug. During the Dow's two-month slide into October, Tokyo's Nikkei index average, a package of 225 stocks, had gained more than three percent. An announcement on October 14 that Shiseido Company, Japan's leading cosmetics manufacturer, had cut its earnings estimates by nearly 50 percent caused some investors to worry. But not much. The Salomon Brothers office in Tokyo forecast that companies in the first section of the Tokyo Stock Exchange, where the blue chips dwell, would see profits grow by a remarkable 26 to 30 percent during the current fiscal year. Although the U.S. and Japanese economies were interlocked in many ways, the Tokyo stock market seemed to be unaffected by Wall Street's declines. "The stock market here doesn't have to follow New York," one analyst in Tokyo said.

Explained Hisanichi Sawa, first vice president of Prudential-Bache Securities (Japan): "The correlation between price movements in New York and price movements in Tokyo is becoming less and less." But soon, Tokyo and New York will fall in tandem.

Ironically, one reason for the optimism in Tokyo was related to U.S. demands that Japan expand its domestic businesses and not rely so much on the export trade that had driven the United States into a deep deficit with the nation it helped rebuild after World War II. The buoyant Tokyo stock market reflected growth in the nation's domestic economy. Stocks related to doing business at home— housing, construction, retail, travel and leisure—were prospering in the Land of the Rising Sun. Several major government enterprises were being privatized. Last winter, Nippon Telephone and Telegraph Corporation made its first stock offering, the most expensive in the world, at about $19,000 for one share. The offering was successful, significantly boosting trading volume on the Tokyo exchange.

In 1986, volume on the Tokyo Stock Exchange averaged 708.6 million shares a day, a whopping 66 percent increase over 1985. In the first four months of 1987, the daily average soared to more than 1.2 billion shares. The Tokyo market was becoming the biggest in the world and feeling proud of itself. Knocking on the door for a seat on the Tokyo exchange, once off-limits to foreigners, were brokerage houses from the United States, Britain, France, West Germany and Switzerland.

While the Tokyo exchange was expanding and New York markets were dropping, the American dollar continued to fall against major trading currencies as a result of Wednesday's pessimistic trade report. Washington put the August trade deficit at $15.7 billion. That was an improvement over July's imbalance of $16.5 billion, a record, but Wall Street had expected an even better showing for August. The deficit with Japan alone was around $5 billion. In Tokyo, the dollar fell nearly two yen. The pound climbed one cent in London, and the dollar also dropped in West Germany, Switzerland, Canada and France. A couple of yen won't buy a cup of tea on Tokyo's Ginza. But world trade is denominated in the billions, and two yen off a dollar makes a mighty hole.

Interest rates climbing. The dollar falling. All bad news. The New York exchange closed at 4 P.M., down by 57.61 points after a brave midday rally. In the last 30 minutes of trading, the Dow Jones plunged more than 53 points, an astounding drop. It was the fourth-busiest day in the history of the New York Stock Exchange: volume 263.2 million shares. Big as it was, today's sales on the New York Exchange were about one billion shares below an average day in Tokyo.

4

Friday, October 16

AFTER THE PAPER-AND-PENCIL AGE

Not too many years ago, Wall Street conducted its business with paper and pencil. Bundles of stocks and bonds were crammed into briefcases and carried from one office to another. Before the computer age, hands, fingers and feet could cope. But if trading volume approached, say, 20 million shares on a single day, fingers and feet were pressed to Olympian speeds. Who, 20 years ago, could have dreamed of Wall Street efficiently conducting 200 million transactions in a single trading day, a tenfold increase over what would have been a crisis level just two decades earlier? Can we increase life expectancy from 72 to 720 years in the next two decades? Some of us hope so. Or perhaps not, depending on how life looks to you.

But hold on! On this Friday, an astounding 344 million shares—equity in the ownership of thousands of corporations that feed, clothe, shelter, fuel, entertain and otherwise serve us—will be traded on Wall Street before the closing bell. Today's trading was the highest single-day volume in the history of the New York Stock Exchange, but still puny when matched against Tokyo.

Said Wall Street telephone clerk David O'Hearn: "The only good thing about the day was that it was Friday."

Said Richard Torrenzano, vice president of the New York Stock Exchange: "The market operated smoothly during its busiest day ever." He explained, "This has a lot to do with the state-of-the-art technology put in place in the last five to seven years." Well, wait until Monday.

Buying and selling securities is an industry that is tailor-made for computers. The products traded on Wall Street are intangible. They can be flashed from buyer to seller through electronic circuits. No packaging required. No wrapping. No delivery service. No return postage requested. "I don't think there was another industry which could have been transformed to the degree the securities industry has been," said Frederic Withington, a New York computer consultant talking with *The Wall Street Journal*. "It's the only one where the goods have no physical reality—they're nothing but an electronic message. So you can move the entire inventory at the stroke of a key." In October 1987, the artists of creative finance did not miss this point.

The Securities Industry Automation Corporation (SIAC) handles electronic trading for the New York and American Stock Exchanges. In 1976, SIAC started what it called the DOT System, an acronym for "designated order turnaround." Now upgraded and called SuperDot, the high-speed network enables member firms to zip electronic orders directly from their traders' computers to a printer on the exchange floor at the speed of light.

Ironically, the word "super" was deleted from the name "SuperDot" after the October crash—and for good reason, as you will see.

Dealing in huge blocks of stocks, program traders found their perfect tool in SuperDot. The system allowed them to place complex orders made up of many stocks and then execute those orders in seconds. In doing so, they could generate a profit on swift price discrepancies between stock prices on Wall Street and their future values as traded in other exchanges.

After computers made possible the exploration of space, powerful models were developed for Wall Street. These computers enabled the securities industry to invent innovative trading techniques designed to lessen a trader's risk in the market and increase, by millions of dollars, his or her potential earning power. More and more, the stock market was becoming a high-speed computer game, more akin to calculating mathematical trading equations than forecasting the fundamentals of the stock-issuing companies: their sales growth, profits and dividends. Not what Exxon will earn in the next quarter, but rather the fractional difference in price between a bundle of stocks on Wall Street and its estimated price in the future as quoted on a Chicago market. Wall Street's computers gave birth to such sophisticated trading innovations as portfolio insurance and index arbitrage that depend on near-instantaneous delivery of information.

Program trading. Portfolio insurance. Index arbitrage. Let us define those terms. Wall Street understood them before October. But to millions of Americans who work and shop on Main Street, program trading was a new puzzle in the mysteries of high finance. Commentators discussed the terms on television screens and in newspaper pages after the October crash, but sometimes not clearly enough for the uninitiated.

Program trading: This umbrella term describes a number of strategies involved in trading a portfolio, or basket, of stocks. Computers are used extensively to sell or buy stocks, options or futures indexes. Computers also enable traders to profit from price differences that develop between two markets, or between a stock index and the price of the underlying stocks that make up that index.

Program trading often attempts to benefit from a window of opportunity that may last only a few minutes. Critical to program trading is accurate and current information, fast trading systems and computers to execute a transaction speedily. Portfolio insurance and index arbitrage, which are explained below, are two widely used applications of program trading. Others include asset reallocation, hedging, cash arbitrage, index substitution and dozens of other varieties with creative buzz names.

Program trading does not mean that computers take over and run the market like a science-fiction robot. Although highly computerized, program trading is designed, managed and controlled by people. Any program-trading tactic can be altered or stopped at any time. The computers do not dominate the system. The traders do. In order to adjust to new market conditions, traders can retune their computer programs at any time. After the October crash, some media and other reports conveyed the impression that the market was locked into computer systems that drove prices down automatically while traders watched in dismay. This impression is not correct. Traders remained in control of the transactions they wanted to make. The computers simply were their tools.

Portfolio insurance: Portfolio insurance refers to trading techniques that are designed to protect stockowners against losses while accepting some limitations on the opportunity to gain. There are dozens of portfolio-insurance strategies. Some of them are kept secret by their operators. All of them are based on the same general tactic. By this tactic, the buying or selling of stocks and futures is triggered when their prices reach preset parameters. Portfolio-insurance strategies usually are carried out by computers. The insurance programs are conducted by simultaneous purchase and sale of stocks, and some basket of stocks, also called indexes, in the futures market.

Here is a description of one widely used portfolio insurance strategy:

When the market drops, large investors—wishing to gain long-term appreciation in the value of their stocks by holding on to them while still minimizing risks—protect their portfolios, not by selling their shares, but instead by selling futures or options that are matched to a well-known stock index such as Standard & Poor's list of 500 shares representing a wide variety of industries. The big boys keep their stocks in their pockets and insure those securities by trading in a statistical index. Here is an example: The market is falling. An investor sells a stock futures index for, let us say, $10,000. He or she does not own that index, so the investor is selling short. The index falls to $8,000. The investor buys it for $8,000 to cover the short sale on which the investor already has collected $10,000. Voila! He or she has earned a profit of $2,000, less a small commission. The investor uses this profit to offset the loss in the stocks without ever touching the stocks. The investor never sold the stocks. He or she kept them safe and secure in the portfolio, and lost no money when the value of that portfolio fell. If the market climbed rather than fell, the investor would lose money on the index transaction, but the stocks in his or her portfolio would have gained in value.

Large institutional investors such as pension funds are heavy players in portfolio insurance. For several years leading up to 1987, portfolio insurance grew rapidly. By October 1987 it covered more than $60 billion in securities, mostly shares owned by pension funds. Brokerage commissions and other costs incurred are cheaper when trading in indexes than when trading in the stocks themselves, another plus for portfolio insurance.

As we will see, portfolio insurance that works under normal conditions unfortunately did not work when it was most needed, in a catastrophic situation. Compare portfolio insurance to an auto policy that fails at the time of an accident.

Index arbitrage: This technique capitalizes on price differences between stock-index futures and the stocks themselves. If index futures become more expensive than the combined expected price of the stocks included in the index, program traders sell the futures and buy the cheaper stocks. When futures fall and stocks rise, they sell the stocks and buy the futures. Price gaps between stocks and futures typically are small and fluctuate rapidly. To realize a profit, index arbitrageurs must execute sales at bullet speeds. The computers that drive the DOT system can trade in minutes as many as 500 separate stock issues worth up to $30 million.

Traditional investors purchase stocks in companies that they believe will perform well and produce growth in future earnings and dividends. They are investing in the nation's economy, its industry, its agriculture, its services and its people. But portfolio insurers and program traders ignore the fundamentals of a business. They do not care what company they buy. They simply are looking for price differences between stocks and futures on which, by carrying out transactions involving tens of thousands of shares, they can make substantial profits on small price differences in minutes or even seconds, or protect their investments against market fluctuations. The long-term future of a corporation or a broad trend in the national economy concerns them not. They are a new breed of deal makers who took over Wall Street just a year or two before the crash. Will they learn a lesson from October?

Former U.S. Attorney General Nicholas deB. Katzenbach, who has made a study of program trading, commented on the present stock market environment—its culture, if you like. "I think there is a tendency today to substitute trading for investment," he said.

From program trading came a vast increase in volume. Millions of shares of stock spewed out of computers at speeds no eye can follow. Questions were raised about orderly markets in October, and the Securities and Exchange Commission (SEC) examined those questions in a detailed study conducted after the crash. The SEC concluded that stock exchanges lacked the ability to handle the record volume of trade during the October crash.

"The record-breaking sell-off during the October market break simply overwhelmed market-making capacity on both the securities and futures markets," the SEC said. "Weaknesses were highlighted in each of the market-making systems: exchange specialists, exchange market-makers, the NASDAQ competitive market-maker systems and the futures markets' open outcry system."

A MISSILE AND A BIOPSY

On this day, Nancy Reagan faced her biopsy bravely. Stoically, she said: "I guess it's my turn."

Where did the missile come from? At Moslem prayers in Teheran, Preident Ali Khamenei of Iran offered his answer: "Where the missile came from, the Almighty knows best."

On this day that was to set the stage for Monday's crash, a pall fell over the Persian Gulf, petroleum reservoir to the world. A missile that the United States believed was fired by Iran escaped a Kuwaiti attempt to shoot it out of the sky and exploded into an oil tanker, the *Sea Isle City*, as it rode at anchor in Kuwaiti territorial waters, wounding several of its crew. Owned by Kuwait, the ship was flying the American flag. It was the first direct attack against one of the 11 Kuwaiti merchant vessels that had registered under a U.S. policy pledging them military protection in the international waters of the Gulf.

In Washington, officials prepared several options for President Reagan's response to the attack. As tensions mounted in the Gulf, some investors rushed their funds into safe Treasury securities and gold stocks climbed, reflecting the traditional trust placed in those financial instruments during periods of domestic or international crisis. Apparently, some investors still feel that the best portfolio insurance is old-fashioned gold.

In its post-October review of the market, the SEC said that the sharp price decline from October 14 through 16, the last trading day before Black Monday, with the Dow Jones Industrial Average falling 235.48 points, "was the result of a variety of factors relating to economic news and fears of an impending market correction. The economic news included continuing problems in the nation's trade deficit and its implications for the federal budget deficit, declines in the value of the U.S. dollar and increases in interest rates."

But not all the news was bad on this morning of October 16. The Labor Department reported that declines in energy prices during September offset increases in food and automobile prices. In

September, gasoline prices fell 6.4 percent and fuel oil dropped 11.4 percent. Food was up 1.1 percent, passenger cars up 3.6 percent. The net result for the month was a modest increase of only three-tenths of one percent in producer prices. Inflation was not in sight. The producer price index is considered to be one of the best leading indicators in predicting inflation rates.

Economics has been called the dismal science, but its practitioners do report some good days. Commenting on the September Labor Department report, Robert L. Marks, president of the New York consulting firm of Siff, Oakley and Marks, said: "I think it supports the view that we are not in the early stages of a sustained acceleration of inflation." But the good news on inflation failed to save Wall Street.

THE FUSE TO BLACK MONDAY

"Without question, there was panic today."

In those words, Rudolph P. Carbone, a vice president of Shearson Lehman Hutton, summed up a historic bench mark on the New York Stock Exchange: October 16, the first day in which the Dow Jones Industrial Average ever lost more than 100 points in a single trading session. The boxscore:

- The Dow Jones fell 108.35 points to 2,247, a 4.6 percent loss for the day, the sixth-highest percentage decline since the end of World War II
- 344 million shares were traded during the day, another new record, exceeding the previous record of 302.4 million shares set on January 22, 1987.
- The loss wiped out $145 billion in stock value, according to the Wilshire Associates' index—a figure equal to almost 15 percent of the entire federal budget for the year.

Friday's losses were so great that market analysts suspected causes other than aches and pains in the national and international economies. Extreme volatility had entered the marketplace in October. The Dow fell 91.6 points on October 6, 95.5 points on October 14, 57.6 points on October 15 and now a new record, shattering the 100-point barrier.

The SEC summed up the month in a rather low-key style: "During October 1987 the nation's securities markets experienced an extraordinary surge of volume and price volatility." In its detailed analysis, the SEC pointed its finger directly toward Friday as the fuse that ignited the next trading day, Black Monday. "The 16th was the DJIA's first 100-point close-to-close decline, a factor which may have played a role in the market psychology of the next week."

The SEC's study identified significant irregularities in the use of portfolio-insurance strategies by institutional investors: a substantial amount of stock selling on October 16 that may have led to massive selling three days later, after the weekend, on Black Monday. "Portfolio-insurance strategies, under normal circumstances," the SEC wrote, "use sales of index futures to reduce equity exposure in order to take advantage of the lower transaction costs in the futures markets. The fact that the alternative of more expensive stock sales were used late on October 16 was a precursor of further stock selling on a massive scale on the 19th."

Thus, Black Monday actually started on Friday.

THE OPENING BELL

Moments after the New York Stock Exchange opened on this Friday morning, 309,500 shares were sold, followed, between 9:30 and 10 A.M., by another 53,300 shares, all part of portfolio-insurance programs. In the same opening hour, three index-arbitrage sell programs were executed involving 2,572,578 shares. The Dow Jones rose 12 points in the first 45 minutes of the trading day, then dropped 13 points in 15 minutes. During those 15 minutes, nine index-arbitrage programs were sold involving 3,010,733 shares. One share in four that was traded from 9:50 to 10 A.M. was tied up in an index-arbitrage deal.

2 P.M.: INTO A FREE-FALL

From 10:11 A.M. to 10:36 A.M., eight program deals were executed, and during that same period the Dow Jones fell by 17.5 points. About 33 percent of the blue-chip stocks sold from 10:20 to 10:30 A.M. were linked to program trading, and 16 percent from 10:30 to 10:40 A.M.

At 11:30 A.M., the Dow Jones average had fallen 28 points in 30 minutes, during which program sales totaled 3,695,700 shares. By noon, the Dow had gained back 22 points, and it added a fraction of a point (0.7) during the next hour. From 1 to 2 P.M., several waves of trading in index-arbitrage programs hit the New York Stock Exchange. In a 60-minute period, 27 program transactions were identified. Program selling accounted for 14 percent of the blue-chip shares traded from 1:40 to 1:50 P.M., and 21 percent during the next ten minutes. When the hour ended, the Dow had lost another 29 points. The precrash free-fall was continuing.

4 P.M.: $300-BILLION LOSS

The computers continued to hum, and a short rally developed. From 2 to 2:30 P.M., 19 index-arbitrage programs were bought or sold in transactions involving 1,912,010 shares. The Dow Jones recovered 38.2 points during this 30-minute period. But program trading did not spark this rally. Stock purchased in index-arbitrage buy programs accounted for only about one percent of the total New York Stock Exchange volume during this period. Apparently some straight investors were fishing for values in the mess, but they bet it wrong because the market was on a long downward slide.

Sales related to portfolio insurance accounted for eight percent of the volume between 2:30 and 3 P.M., and the Dow Jones lost approximately 11 points.

At 3:20 P.M. the Dow had lost another 23 points. During the last 30 minutes of the trading day, sales turned into a blizzard. More than 53 million shares were transacted—29,444 shares a second. Transactions conducted in that 30-minute period, with computers spinning, totaled more than double what the market could have handled in a normal trading day 20 years earlier. "Arbitrage-related sales of stocks were heaviest as the Dow Jones dropped over 50 points from 3:30 to 3:50, and abated somewhat as the market recovered points thereafter," the SEC said. In that 20-minute period, sales related to arbitrage totaled 9,350,000 shares, and 1.7 million shares were sold in portfolio-insurance strategies.

When this last trading day before Black Monday ended at 4 P.M., three new records were written in the ledgers: The Dow's greatest one-day point drop in history, 108.35 points; the first time ever for a decline of more than 100 points in a single day; and the exchange's heaviest daily volume ever, 344 million shares.

"A bad and busy day," one trader told us.

During the week now ended, the value of U.S. corporate stocks had plunged more than $300 billion.

This record plunge may well have played a significant role in the market psychology of the week to come. In one day, the Dow had lost 4.6 percent of its value.

From a peak of 2,722 points on August 25, the Industrial Average had dropped to 2,246 points, shedding a frightening 17.5 percent of its value.

It was not widely noticed that the 1987 market break actually was divided into two phases roughly of equal magnitude. A relatively gradual decline of 476 points in the Dow Jones Industrial Average took place over 52 volatile days and then a swift plunge of 508 points happened on one day. Thus, if not black like Monday, the end of summer in 1987 at least was bleak.

A TELEPHONE CALL FROM TOKYO

On this Friday before the crash, one of the authors of this book attended a lunch of the Financial Management Association in Las Vegas, Nevada. The guest speaker was T. Boone Pickens, the Texas billionaire. While he was eating, Pickens lost about $2 million on Wall Street, but it seemed not to bother him in the least. Oh, for the life of the rich!

Later, on a television call-in show after the crash, Pickens commented on the record-high level of stock prices before Black Monday. "You keep loading the wagon until the axle breaks," he said. He went on to say that the general economy remained in good shape and noted, among other things, that the nation's unemployment was down to 5.9 percent, its lowest level since 1979. "There are lots of jobs out there, although maybe not the job you want." He demonstrated faith in an old-fashioned disaster hedge with one answer to a question: "Gold? I'm in it big." He expressed confidence that Black Monday would not lead to a depression. "This crash bears no relation to 1929. In 1929 they jumped out of windows." Would you jump out a window? "No, I've got low blood pressure."

Two months earlier, the same author was in Japan on a lecture trip. One night in his Tokyo hotel he was worried because he feared that stock prices had climbed to their highest possible level and now could only decline. He got out of bed and telephoned his broker in the United States, where it was daytime. His order: Sell all my stocks.

NITROGLYCERINE AND WINE

Portfolio insurance was invented, not on Wall Street, but by professors of finance whose salaries are insured by lifetime tenure. Professors whose teaching and research is academically sound and whose writings are accepted by scholarly journals are rewarded by their universities with the coveted status of tenure, employment for life. Years ago, the charismatic Sukarno of Indonesia, who could hold audiences spellbound while he orated for hours, declared himself president for life. Unfortunately, he was deposed. Not so in the ivy-covered buildings on university campuses.

Unless they commit a crime, which professors seldom seem to do, members of the tenured faculty do not lose their sinecure. When they reach 65 or 70 they become professors emeritus and live off funds provided by the largest pension system in the United States, the Teachers Insurance and Annuity Association and the College Retirement Equities Fund. In 1987, assets of the two funds totaled $60.7 billion.

In a 1987 interview, a distinguished professor of finance at an Ivy League universisty, who had lectured to financiers in the United States and Europe, outlined for a news reporter the complex mathematical formulas that he had designed to explain precisely what certain financial markets will do in the future.

"How much money have you made on the stock market?" the reporter asked.

"None," the doctor of philosophy replied. "I never invest in Wall Street. A successful investor must be able to monitor the market daily, and I can't do that from the classroom. And besides, I need the perspective of distance to conduct my research."

Fair enough. But, remote from the split-second decisions that sweating traders make on the Big Board, mathematical formulas were computed in the quiet of a scholar's study, and Wall Street's largest investors adopted those equations to protect their portfolios. The idea was textbook simple: insure stocks by trading in the anticipated future value of those securities. Don't sell shares. Instead, when stock prices fell on Wall Street protect your portfolios by selling financial index futures on the Chicago Mercantile Exchange. When you sell short, you make money when prices go down. Thus, portfolio insurers cover stock losses by generating profits on falling indexes. It's a no-loss game, like a doctor who owns a funeral home on the side.

To accomplish this trick, program traders usually trade in the Standard and Poor's Index, which is a basket of 500 of the nation's most highly followed stocks. By Black Monday more than $135 billion-dollars' worth of portfolios were protected by this university-invented system of insurance.

Program trading and other futures index transactions have become so widespread in recent years that the underlying market value of index futures traded daily generally exceeds the dollar volume on the New York Stock Exchange. This has been the case in all daily transactions since the last quarter of 1983. Not too many people realize that a large part of Wall Street moved in recent years to the futures market in Chicago.

Four months before Black Monday, a group of financial academics and three members of the Securities and Exchange Commission, created during the Great Depression to protect the investing public against malpractice in securities markets, met in a conference at the University of Rochester. Recalling this meeting, David Dreman, a Wall Street investment counsel, wrote in *Forbes* magazine one month after Black Monday: "I sat on a panel [at Rochester] discussing the dangers of program trading and portfolio insurance. I expressed my concern about a potential crash through the misuse of these instruments. The professors treated me rather condescendingly. They said, in effect, that we Wall Street people just didn't understand markets."

Dreman casts himself as a prophet. Months before the Rochester meeting, he wrote in *Forbes:* "What looks good in the lab can act like nitroglycerine when shaken."

The first Wall Street crisis to test academic theories of portfolio insurance was the stock market crash of October 1987. This was the first acid test, the moment of truth. The October explosion suggested that a high grade of nitroglycerine was involved. Until Black Monday, portfolio insurance indeed did protect stocks. During moderate price declines that, on occasion, interrupted the roaring bull market that swept Dow Jones Industrial Averages to their highest levels in history, stocks were defended neatly by portfolio insurance. But in October, when the professorial theories faced their first grueling test, many big investors tossed the mathematical formulas out the window and went back to the simplest defense against a falling market: They sold their stocks.

Thus, portfolio insurance failed faster than a first-year student going into final exams without cracking a book all semester. The system flopped, not because of errors in the scholarly formulas, but because Wall Street's then-record decline during the week that ended on October 16 struck fear into the hearts of several major investors. Portfolio insurance never had been tested in a crisis. Unwilling to experiment further, some portfolio insurers decided to abandon the academic approach and sell stocks in massive quantities. Other investors followed suit.

It was this dismantling of program trading that accelerated the crash, not program trading itself. Program trading requires accurate market information, speedy execution of transactions, a continuous market and non-erratic price movements—conditions that failed during the crisis. Also, portfolio insurance cannot accomodate all traders at the same time.

Let's Save Our Necks

We can picture a scene in a future year. It's Friday evening. The New York Stock Exchange closed at 4 P.M. The Dow Jones had been battered by its deepest one-day decline in history, far greater than in 1987. Selling volume was insane. Over 800 million shares were traded, the highest volume since the exchange was founded in the eighteenth century. Much of the selling was suspected to have been done by portfolio-insurance managers. When everybody is selling at the same time, portfolio insurance does not work. And this time it was dead. The big-money folks had lost confidence in portfolio insurance.

Three traders for a major mutual fund occupy a corner table in an Italian restaurant. The pasta is excellent. But they regret their risk of the evening: a Fingers Lake wine from upstate New York.

"I told you we should have at least ordered a California red. The market isn't so bad that we have to drop down to this New York crap. I never did like this restaurant. We should have gone to that Chinese place around the corner and tried their mao-tai. That stuff is pure lightning."

"Come on. We got a hell of a lot more to worry about than the wine list in this place. If those bastards keep selling on Monday, we're going to get creamed before the boss gets to the office. We better start moving, and fast."

"OK. I couldn't believe what I saw today. Our system should have held. It always worked in the past. But it sure as shit didn't today."

"Man, in that kind of volatile market it can't work. Before the order is executed, the price changes and reverses the reason for the trade."

"True. The information we were getting was lousy. I couldn't read the market. It was such a mess today that I couldn't tell up from down."

"What if the computer system collapses? I can't do program trading with an abacus."

"I don't like it. There's nothing like this in the book."

"Well, we ain't got too many options."

"Hell, we ain't got any options. Actually, it ain't that bad. This year has been pretty good to us. Let's save our necks in the old-fashioned way: Cut your losses, sell the stocks at any price. Forget about portfolio insurance. It can't work now."

"You're right. Hey, Luigi, let me have another look at that wine list."

To an extent satisfied, the three traders try an Italian red and, along with many others, abandon program trading and sell several hundred million dollars' worth of stock on a future Black Day.

5

The Weekend

SATURDAY, OCTOBER 17: JOGGING IN A VOLATILE MARKET

In a 50-minute operation, surgeons at Bethesda Naval Hospital removed Nancy Reagan's left breast, where a small cancer had been detected. The prognosis was good: recovery without complications. "Honey, I know you don't feel like dancing," President Reagan said. "So let's hold hands."

Reagan, a cancer victim himself, had dealt with health problems that would challenge the bravest. And now the smoke from Wall Street appeared to be darkening the president's optimistic assessment of the nation's economy under his administration.

Down in Midland, Texas, doctors reported that little Jessica McClure, bruised on her foot and forehead, was doing nicely after the end to her ordeal in an abandoned well.

And in New York City, Barrett N. Sinowitz, a stockbroker for Prudential-Bache Securities, discussed jogging as a market barometer. He told reporter Andrew Feinberg of *The New York Times* that he runs more when the markets are volatile. "This has been an absolutely wonderful year for jogging," he commented. "I'm now doing so much that I've entered the New York Marathon."

No one lives on Wall Street. Except for tourists, perhaps a few clerks, an occasional computer technician, security guards changing shifts, crews that sweep away the trash—and a few weekend

51

joggers—New York's financial district is deserted from Friday night until Monday morning. But the forces that drive the market do not rest even on weekends.

Treasury Secretary James A. Baker appeared on the Cable News Network program, "Newsmaker Saturday." Because of its contributions to the stock market crash, Baker's interview may have been one of history's most expensive TV shows. He continued his attacks, started a few days earlier, on West German interest rates with comments that many analysts believe played a substantial role in the October crash. A 1957 law school graduate from the University of Texas, Baker, 57, and his wife Susan are parents of eight children. Baker was undersecretary in the Department of Commerce when Gerald Ford was president, and White House chief of staff under Reagan before moving to the Treasury Department. Most certainly, he spoke for the president on critical economic issues.

On Cable News Network, Baker discussed the past week on Wall Street, during which the Dow Jones suffered its biggest weekly loss since World War II, 235 points. After the Dow peaked in August, the market plunge had wiped out almost $500 billion in stock prices before Black Monday. In comparison, stock losses through the first three years of the Great Depression, 1929 to 1931, totaled only $50 billion.

On TV, Baker defended the American economy: "I think if you look at the underlying economic fundamentals in this country, they're very, very good." He agreed with analysts that computerized trading programs played an important role in the market's decline during the previous week. Baker was conducting good politics with investors. They needed reassurances on the economy. And blaming a scapegoat, program trading in this case, rather than the nation's basic economic ills, may help calm a stormy market. But, unfortunately, Baker did not stop there. On this critical weekend, the secretary of the Treasury had a lot to say on West German interest rates. In doing so, he made headlines that were read around the world. Assuredly, Baker helped to apply black paint to the coming Monday.

Earlier in the week, Baker had called newspeople in for a briefing in Washington during which he criticized recent increases in German interest rates. The arguments had been made before. Higher interest rates in Germany could hurt both the United States and Germany. The German domestic economy would decline, because higher interest rates would make it more expensive to borrow capital funds to expand the economy at home. Higher rates would encourage German consumers to deposit their surplus income in banks or bonds and spend less, thus depressing their purchases, including products made in America.

On Saturday's national television program, Baker seized the opportunity to repeat his comments, chastising the Germans for allowing their interest rates to climb. The repetition multiplied the impact. The message was clear. Although he did not mention the U.S. dollar by name (government officials can ignite panics in the marketplace by suggesting devaluation), Baker was telling Germany and the world that the United States might allow the dollar to decline even further against the West German mark as a retaliation against higher German interest rates. A cheaper dollar would shrink profits on German goods sold in the United States.

Baker argued that interest increases in Germany, although less than one percent, ran counter to the monetary agreement signed in France's historic Louvre Palace in February by the seven industrial powers of the West—Britain, France, West Germany, Italy, Canada, the United States and Japan. Those nations are known as the Group of Seven, or G-7. In Paris, eight months earlier, ministers of the G-7 nations said they would maintain stable exchange rates, Germany and Japan would try harder to develop their economies at home, and the United States would reduce its budget deficit.

Brave words. Under the Louvre terms, Germany and Japan would retarget their national economies to produce more construction projects, merchandise and services for domestic consumption rather than rely so heavily on the exports that were driving the United States into debt. But, argued Baker, you don't expand a national economy by hiking interest rates. Rate increases negate every kind of spending, from credit-card purchases to factory expansion, and play havoc with the stock market.

Baker had another message. He told Americans who tuned in on Saturday that Wall Street losses appeared to be reactions to several factors, including possible tax increases, proposed legislation to limit foreign imports, and fears of inflation and rising interest rates. His litany was a complete checklist of all economic evils.

When government officials tinker with just one millimeter of the economy, investors respond with whiplash speed. Standard reactions include:

- If interest rates climb, business will be depressed.
- If the dollar falls against other currencies, inflation follows because prices will increase on imported automobiles, clothing and electronic goods. Already inflation had picked up slightly, although still negligible, while the dollar declined 40 percent from its February 1985 peak.
- If barriers are erected against foreign products, American manufacturers will hike prices at home. Lacking foreign competition, product quality and productivity will suffer in U.S. industries.
- If taxes increase, what's left to spend?

Evidently stock markets in London, Tokyo and New York interpreted Secretary Baker's comments as a signal that Washington would permit the value of the U.S. dollar to fall. In this, investors saw significant problems with the U.S. economy, despite its high employment, increasing productivity and negligible inflation. Even worse, a falling dollar would lower the income that foreign investors could expect to earn from American securities, encouraging foreigners to decrease their sizable investments in the American market.

The last thing Wall Street needed after its past traumatic week was another dose of pessimism administered by a top government official.

In comments published on Sunday in *The New York Times* and, no doubt, read at home by many Wall Street players, Felix Rohatyn, a senior partner of Lazard Freres and Company, said that a decline in the dollar "could reinforce weakness in the stock market." He explained: "Foreign holders will bail out of stocks to bail out of our currency. You have to look at the dollar, not just in context of the trade market, but in the context of the capital market as well."

Wall Street is fueled by perceptions. Pessimism, justified or not, can create black days on the Big Board.

SUNDAY, OCTOBER 18: BLAME IT ON THE GERMANS

Headlines in *The New York Times* and *The Wall Street Journal*, reporting Sunday's news developments, telegraphed both pessimism and optimism to Wall Street's movers and shakers as they skimmed Monday-morning newspapers while riding the commuter trains and subways to Black Monday:

In the Aftermath of Market Plunge, Much Uneasiness

Reagan Chooses the U.S. Response to Iranian Attack

The Economy and Stocks: Separate but Linked

Some Stay Bullish, Believing Downturn Is Temporary;
"Bears Are Running Wild"

An Appraisal: Enormous Volume Could Be a Good Sign, Some Say

Many Bankers Seem Reluctant to Follow Chemical's Lead in Lifting
Prime Rate

On such reports, markets rise and fall.

Secretary Baker was determined to get across his message to Germany. For the third time in four days, he went public on his warnings against an increase in West German interest rates. Appearing on NBC's "Meet the Press" program on Sunday, the Treasury secretary spoke with an even greater emphasis than his rhetoric of Thursday and Saturday: "We will not sit back in this country and watch surplus countries jack up· their interest rates and squeeze growth worldwide on the expectation that the United States somehow will follow by raising its interest rates."

In his own analysis of the turmoil on Wall Street, Baker did not limit himself to interest rates. He put part of the problem in the laps of congressional committee members who then were preparing tax legislation for the 1988 federal budget. "I think the writing of these tax packages had a major effect on what's happening to the stock market over the course of the past three or four days," Baker said. The secretary drew a quick retort from Senator Lloyd Bentsen, chairman of the Senate Finance Committee and later to become the Democratic Party's 1988 nominee for vice president. Said Bentsen: "The reason the stock market is dropping is that you've had major banks raising the prime interest rate and concern about the trade deficit and concern about the budget deficit. They blame everybody else—Congress, the Germans, the Japanese."

Washington was preparing to move on another front, this one in the Persian Gulf against Iran for its missile attack on Friday against a Kuwaiti oil tanker flying the U.S. flag. But mum's the word. Asked by reporters if he had selected one of the options prepared by his advisers for retaliation, the president replied: "I've made it." What will it be? "I can't tell you."

Uncertainty never helps Wall Street.

CLOUDS OVER THE ORIENT

The trading day on Far Eastern stock exchanges takes place while Wall Street sleeps. In recent years, telephones have been ringing more often in the middle of the night, awakening bulls and bears from their sleep in New York, Connecticut and New Jersey with calls from Tokyo and Hong Kong, 12 hours away. For good reason. In its postcrash report, the SEC discussed how the major stock markets of the world are affecting each other's operations.

"The October market break highlighted the growing interconnections among securities markets internationally," the SEC wrote. "Ripple effects of the market volatility were seen in strong, well-capitalized international markets such as London and Tokyo, as well as in fast-growing, more speculative markets such as the Hong Kong Exchange, which closed for the week of October 19 [after Monday]. Review of international trading by the SEC's Office of the Chief Economist shows that stock price changes in various markets were significantly correlated and that the United States appeared to lead other markets during this period."

So on Sunday night and on into early Monday, while Wall Street slept or sleepily answered the telephone from Tokyo, most Asian markets plunged in reaction to Friday's record drop on Wall Street:

Tokyo: The Nikkei average of 225 stocks fell 620 points, 2.3 percent of its value.

Hong Kong: The Hang Seng index dropped 421 points, 11.3 percent of its value.

Singapore: The Straits Times index slipped 169 points, 12.1 percent of its value.

Kuala Lumpur: The composite index closed down 51 points, 12.4 percent of its value.

Sydney: The All Ordinaries index declined 80 points, 3.7 percent of its value.

But markets rose in Seoul by a fraction under one percent, in Taipei by 3.2 percent, Bangkok by one percent and Manila by 6.9 percent.

The stage was set for Black Monday.

6

Monday, October 19

"WE'RE TALKING D DAY"

For New York City today, the forecast called for clouds and a high temperature between 58 and 63 degrees Fahrenheit, down from Sunday's 70. The weather forecast was wrong. Monday's high was 68. What about forecasts on Wall Street? Exceedingly nervous, the future uncertain. But for Bernard H. Goetz, the judgment was in and the waiting ended. He was sentenced today to six months in jail for carrying an unlicensed pistol that was used in the December 1984 shooting of four young men on a New York City subway train.

Is Europe important to American finance? Well, for high-school students, New York State educators suggested this morning that learning less European history is good. A new social studies program will place more emphasis on twentieth-century American history, and less on Europe's past. The idea is to help the increasing number of Asian and Hispanic students better understand the heritage of their new homeland. Fine. But, as it has since the nineteenth century, Europe continues to be a major player in the U.S. economy. In *A History of the English-Speaking People,* Winston S. Churchill wrote that in its industrial development after the Civil War "America could look to Europe for capital as well as labour. The bulk of her industrial capital came from British, Dutch and German investors." European money helped build the great railroads, mills, factories and mines that made the United States the world's leading industrial nation until Japan fine-tuned its production.

For Japan on this Monday, a new prime minister was selected. Noboru Takeshita, a former English teacher who speaks almost no English, was picked to succeed Yasuhiro Nakasone, whose term was expiring. In a nation where first names rarely are used, Nakasone prided himself on establishing a Yasu-Ron relationship with the man in the White House. But not all Americans looked upon the Japanese as friends. A view prevailed that the United States was losing sales and manufacturing jobs to Honda, Toyota, Nissan, Sony, NEC, Hitachi, Mitsubishi, Cannon, Kawasaki, Pentel, Bridgestone, Casio and a string of other companies in a land once known to the West primarily for its cherry blossoms, cheap toys and geishas. Several U.S. Representatives demonstrated their wrath by taking up sledgehammers near the steps of the Capitol building and pounding Japanese computers to smithereens.

In Japan, Yasu had dismayed many of his fellow citizens, who continued to call him Nakasone, by permitting military spending, for the first time since World War II, to exceed one percent of Japan's total industrial, agricultural and service production. The increase amounted to only a tiny fraction of one percentage point. But memories of war hang heavy in Japan. The prewar Industry Promotion Hall—gutted, its steel-frame dome rusted, roof tiles melted into shapeless gobs—still stands, a skeleton silhouetted against the sky, as a permanent monument to peace. The building was at the epicenter of the Hiroshima atomic bomb, called by Japanese *genshi bakudan*, "original child bomb," because its force came from nature's original matter. The bomb obliterated every building and house within an area of four square miles. But, perhaps ironically, the four-story hall that was dedicated to Japan's industrial growth stood proud, though wounded, when Emperor Hirohito surrendered his nation to the allied powers. Low-keyed and cautious, Japan's new conservative party leader put a priority on improving his nation's trade balance with the United States. In a typically Japanese political understatement, Takeshita said on this day of crashing stock markets, "I'll try my best."

There was no peace in the Persian Gulf on this morning that was to disintegrate into Black Monday. At about 7 A.M., New York time, two hours and 30 minutes before the markets opened, the military option selected by President Reagan went into action. Retaliating against Iran's attack on an American-defended tanker, four U.S. Navy destroyers shelled and destroyed two connected offshore oil platforms that Iran had converted into a military command center. Fortunately, Arabs in the oil-flushed Persian Gulf generally supported the United States. "I woke up this morning to very good news, the news of your attack on an Iranian platform," Crown Prince Abdullah of Saudi Arabia, who was visiting Washington, told President Reagan.

That was perhaps the only good news the President heard on this Monday.

After prices plunged on Asia's stock exchanges and before New York markets opened for Monday's transactions, the international ripples, as they were called by the SEC—or were they waves?—washed over Europe with heavy selling on all markets. The *Financial Times* index of 30 shares in London fell by 183.7 points, a 10.1 percent plunge, and its 100-share index dropped 249.6 points to 2,053.3.

"We're talking D Day," said Franklin Craig at Cerepfi, a Paris brokerage house. While hardly comparable to the Allied landings on Normandy in World War II, the major index on the Paris market slumped 4.65 percent. Luis Felipe Santo Domingo, a Merrill Lynch investment adviser in the French capital, said: "People are calling to ask whether it's going to be like 1929." On the floors of stock exchanges in Milan, Stockholm, Amsterdam, Brussels, Frankfurt and Zurich, declines ranged from six to 11 percent.

Treasury Secretary Baker's recent comments on West German interest rates had led European and Asian bankers to fear that the United States would permit the dollar to fall, not only against the market, but against other major trading currencies as well. A devalued dollar would increase the price of foreign goods in America, making it more difficult for exporting nations such as West Germany and Japan to sell. And a cheaper dollar would decrease the earnings of foreign investors holding U.S.-dollar stocks and bonds.

The dollar was in a mess, and Europeans, big investors in America since the nineteenth century, said so on Black Monday.

"Over here in Europe, there was only one move made by investors—sell the dollars," said Hans-Joerg Rudloff, a general manager in Credit Suisse, Switzerland's third-largest bank. "The seriousness of the U.S. problem as a debtor nation hasn't been seen yet. The stock market decline is a symptom. The big bucks will get lost in the foreign-exchange markets. Hundreds of billions of dollars could leave the United States."

Analysts of the crash clearly recognized the impact of trading abroad on U.S. stocks. In its postcrash study, the Securities and Exchange Commission wrote that on October 19 "The [New York, American and Chicago Mercantile] markets' turmoil was evidenced first in heavy selling on foreign markets prior to the opening of trading in the United States."

MINTING SUPERLATIVES

In the first paragraph of its lead article on page one in Tuesday's edition, *The Wall Street Journal* avoided a common error of newspaper writers who sometimes are inclined to embellish momentous events with monumental phrases. In five words *The Journal* told it all:

NEW YORK—The stock market crashed today.

Even the Securities and Exchange Commission in its report, couched for the most part in deathly dull prose, opened with the simplicity of Abraham Lincoln at Gettysburg. In its October trading chronology, the SEC introduced Black Monday with these words:

On Monday, October 19, 1987, the nation's securities and index futures markets suffered their worst decline in history.

But who can resist superlatives when history is created? So let us record a few that we will see unfolding on this Black Monday:

- The Dow Jones Industrial Average collapsed by 508.32 points to close at 1,738.40, shattering every record in the book.
- The Dow's nosedive, a 22.6 percent loss, was almost twice the percentage drop on October 29, 1929, in the twilight before the Great Depression. The 1929 decline was 12.82 percent.
- The 608 million shares transacted on Monday on the New York Stock Exchange nearly doubled the previous all-time record, set just one trading day earlier, on Friday.
- Monday's massacre destroyed more than $500 billion in the equity value of U.S. stocks. Since summer, the worth of American securities had shriveled by $1 trillion.

A new superlative was added to the lexicon of finance by none other than the chairman of the New York Stock Exchange, John J. Phelan, Jr., when he said, "It's the nearest thing to a meltdown I ever want to see."

The crash of Black Monday started even before the New York markets opened at 9:30 A.M. The fuse had been ignited at least a week earlier in America, and, because of time differences, Monday's record-breaking selling started abroad.

The plunge began in tumultuous markets across the seas and was fueled in America by fears that had built up in investors' minds during the weekend after Friday's nightmare. "Sell orders from abroad were arriving on our desk here in New York at eight o'clock this morning," said Bernard Spilko, senior vice president of Bank Julius Baer of Zurich.

The SEC described Monday's "near-panic selling" as a reflection of "the negative investor sentiment created over the previous week."

Wall Street long had expected the market to cool and prices to fall. By mid-October, before Black Monday, many investors believed that the decline starting in August had reduced stocks to realistic price levels. The worst was over, they reasoned. But, as the U.S. General Accounting Office—the congressional watchdog—reported, other traders "realized that pressure had built over the weekend for a major trading day on Monday, October 19." They were correct.

COLLAPSE OF THE SPECIALISTS' SYSTEM

Specialists on the New York Stock Exchange knew before they got out of bed on Monday that they were headed for trouble.

"Today we are going to witness the greatest calamity ever in the marketplace," Chairman James J. Maguire told his colleague when he arrived for work at Henderson Brothers, a Wall Street specialist firm.

Specialists, sometimes called the buyers of last resort, enable the New York Stock Exchange to function. When no other traders are willing to purchase stock offered for sale, exchange rules require that the specialists buy the shares. Fifty-five specialist firms operate in the New York Stock Exchange. Specific stocks are assigned to each specialist to buy and sell in such a way as to maintain an orderly market. They are called specialists because each of them specializes in stocks assigned exclusively to them. Shrewd trading can earn big profits for specialists. But in return for exclusive trading privileges on the floor, specialists undertake awesome responsibilities. When the market falls, they are required to purchase shares at prices that hopefully will stabilize the market and prevent precipitous declines. They must bend against the wind to maintain an orderly market. In terms of staff, many specialist firms are small organizations. Some of them have been family-owned for generations. To maintain stock inventories, they often rely on borrowed money.

The capital that specialists are required to maintain is singularly modest, Lilliputian by Wall Street standards. Until ten years ago, the New York Stock Exchange required that specialists possess a minimum of $500,000 in capital. Unbelievably, this requirement was reduced in 1977 to only $100,000. Still specialists buy and sell stock in the millions of dollars.

Because they are required to purchase stock almost instantly when no other buyers step forward, specialists need a lot of ready cash and a good line of credit. But in no way are specialists the cash-richest operators on Wall Street—quite the contrary. They are among the poorest.

Funds available to specialists are insignificant when compared to the capital controlled by the upstairs firms. So called because they operate outside the stock market floor, upstairs firms are the major investment houses that normally conduct most of the buying and selling on the stock exchange. They are the superwealthy traders: the Merrill Lynches, the Shearson Lehman Huttons and the Prudential-Baches of Wall Street. Specialists, while possessing more limited funds than the upstairs firms, are required by stock exchange rules to take over trading when the rich upstairs firms are not clearing the market. Upstairs firms can trade as they see fit, beholden only to their customers and to themselves. They are not required by law, regulation or tradition to maintain an orderly market. Actually, they work for themselves. As long as upstairs firms clear the market by agreeing on trading prices that leave no excess buyers or sellers, everything is fine and a continuous market prevails. The role of the specialist then becomes minimal. But that was not the case during the crash. The SEC reported that two specialists told them that during the Monday-Tuesday crisis "upstairs market-making activity evaporated, straining the capacity of the specialists to make orderly markets." Even in a crashing market, brokerage houses should feel some obligation to handle orders from their customers so as to maintain a good business relationship. But the profit focus of brokers changed in the 1980s. In recent years, the big upstairs firms have been earning more money by trading for their own house accounts, formerly a sideline activity, than from commissions earned in handling the transactions of their customers. By becoming major stock market players for their own profit, a possible conflict of interest has developed between brokers and their customers.

One month after the October crash, *Forbes* magazine asked the question, "Whose side is the broker on?" The magazine added: "For the past few years, brokerage houses have generated more revenues—and more profit—by trading for their own accounts than from commissions. Given this pattern, it should come as no surprise that among the biggest practitioners of program trading are the brokerage houses themselves."

The specialist system failed during the October crash. Investors dumped millions of shares for sale on the stock market floor. Specialists could find few buyers. With no formal obligation to purchase and market prices crashing, the wealthy and highly capitalized upstairs firms could sit back and wait for the panic to subside. And so they did. But specialists were stuck. If no other buyers appeared, the stock exchange expected them to purchase shares offered for sale. Stocks were losing value by the second, the market was crashing and specialists were unable to plug the drain no matter how hard they tried. Millions of dollars drained out of specialists' pockets, and some of them were penniless before the market hit bottom. Upstairs firms looked the other way.

In normal times, specialists are able to match buyers with sellers so that trading can be carried out smoothly. They had done so for many years by gradually raising or reducing stock prices and consequently inticing buy or sell orders. If orders were not enough to clear the market, specialists bought or sold for their own accounts. In normal times, the system worked. But during the crash, the flood of sales was so great that no price reductions could offset it. The financial assets of specialists were inadequate to handle a crisis.

"The specialist system did not assume that specialists would engage in unlimited buying and selling to correct any magnitude of imbalance," the SEC said in its post-October study. "Rather, it assumed that specialists' trading would be sufficient to keep the markets orderly and continuous. Upstairs firm activity . . . was regarded as providing an additional source of liquidity to the specialists, an activity that became more important with the increasing institutionalization of the market.

"During the market break, these assumptions did not work. Specialists were confronted with extraordinary imbalances [between sellers and buyers] that required unprecedented capital commitments and the upstairs firms did not provide the aniticipated liquidity."

What worked in normal times did not work under catastrophic conditions, and the stock market collapsed on the shoulders of the specialists. Their duty was to bring order out of chaos, to establish an orderly pricing of shares when everyone was selling and only the brave or foolhardy were buying. That's like trying to get a decent price for a used car with battered fenders and a dragging exhaust pipe. The SEC defines the role of the specialist this way: "The specialists' responsibilities to trade do not require them to stem general downward or upward price movements, but only to temper sudden price movements and keep any general price movements orderly." That's fine on a calm day. But when the earthquake strikes and buildings crack open, who's going to walk down the stairs in an orderly fashion?

From last week's selling deluge and price plunge, specialists knew they faced a market that could cremate their assets before lunch. Rule 104 of the New York Stock Exchange's Constitution and Rules says that the function of a specialist includes "the maintenance, in so far as reasonably practical, of a fair and orderly market on the Exchange in the stocks in which he is so acting."

During the crash, specialists found a saving loophole for themselves in the rule's wording: ". . .so far as reasonably practical." After all, why should they consider themselves to be the buyers of last resort when uncontrolled selling floods the trading floor and the mammoth upstairs firms don't chip in? When the market is crashing at the rate of millions of dollars per second, with no end in sight, specialists simply lack the capital to rein in the avalanche by becoming massive buyers. These are not "reasonable" conditions.

So at the moment of truth, on Monday and Tuesday, when specialists were needed the most, the system did not work. Some specialists decided to save their own necks. They folded their arms and did not perform in the market. "Why should we commit suicide?" one specialist said. "After all, we are not government employees, the fiancial soldiers of the nation." Other specialists performed bravely in attempting to brake the market. But they failed. The forces driving prices down were too powerful. Was it really the specialists' fault, or the fault of a system that never was designed for extreme conditions?

During the 1987 crash, the mechanism that operates financial markets collapsed even more than did the prices. The lesson for the future is clear.

9:30 A.M.: TRAGIC MISCALCULATIONS

From its first minutes, tragic miscalculations made Monday a day to sell, and to sell in record volume. Panic started not in New York, but in the Chicago Mercantile Exchange. For five years, the Mercantile had traded in stock-index futures, which are bought and sold by, among others, owners of large stock portfolios, such as pension funds. They deal in indexes to protect the value of their securities. Indexes, rather than the stocks themselves, are traded on speculation and as a hedge against falling stock prices. It is cheaper to deal in indexes than in stocks, and profits earned on indexes can help cover price losses on stocks in a declining market. Shortly before the October crash, this technique was given a name that had not yet been published in financial textbooks: portfolio insurance.

Within seconds after Chicago opened, one of the major stock-index futures, the Standard & Poor's 500, sank by 20.75 points. That was more than the index had fallen all day on Friday. One large firm was said to have sold more than $600 million in stock-index futures in the first hour of trading.

But, amazingly, the calculations that launched that opening wave of selling were based on guesswork. The index figures that set the most critical opening trend of the day probably were incorrect. If accurate figures had been available shortly after the market opened, Black Monday might have been only gray or not colored at all. The index futures sold in Chicago's early trading were computed, in part, by using the prices at which stocks closed on Friday. The indexes did not reflect Monday's stock prices because very few transactions actually took place when the market opened. This dearth of transactions was caused by large order imbalances and delays in opening specific stocks. Current stock prices can be posted only after that stock is traded. The accuracy of Monday's opening indexes was destroyed, because they were fleshed out with stale indexes left over from Friday. Yet traders accepted those indexes with enough confidence to set in motion the greatest selling binge in Wall Street's history.

The Presidential Task Force, appointed by President Reagan immediately after the crash to investigate its causes, explained the illusory nature of trading information and why investors relied on it: "Since many of the stocks in the index had yet not opened, the index was calculated from their Friday closing prices. Although the index arbitrageurs clearly knew that many stocks had not yet opened, they nevertheless believed that a large discount existed [between the index and the prices of the stocks it represented]. This belief led the index arbitrageur to conclude that the market was headed much lower."

At the same time, by relying on an apparent discount that may not have existed, buyers were discouraged from entering the market, and sales orders piled up with no takers. Thus, Monday's big crash was launched, not by the accurate and reliable information that is essential to effective trading, but by perceptions based on guesswork. Unfortunately, this pattern of operating on half-baked information continued throughout the crisis.

10 A.M.: SPECIALISTS UNDER FIRE

While indexes were being sold in Chicago, stock specialists on the floor of the New York Stock Exchange were overwhelmed with a deluge of orders to sell shares. But few investors were willing to buy. During the first hour, 95 blue-chip stocks failed to open for trading. Specialists could find no buyers. Those stranded shares represented 30 percent of the Standard & Poor's 500 index value.

When the market opened, specialists were forced to reduce prices on stocks they handled by substantial sums in an effort to attract other buyers. For example, 273,700 shares of Coca-Cola were traded for the first time at 9:53 A.M. at $36\frac{1}{4}$, a price that was $3\frac{1}{2}$ points below Friday's close. In other words, the specialist cut the price of Coca-Cola nearly ten percent to find buyers. At 10:40 A.M., Eastman Kodak opened with a trade of 398,400 shares at $76 per share, $13\frac{1}{2}$ points lower than Friday's close. Exxon opened seven minutes later with 1.38 million shares at $40, down $3\frac{1}{2}$ points from the previous close.

The specialist for American Express stock opened at a price down more than two points from Friday. But even with that price reduction he was forced to buy 150,000 shares himself, because there were not enough other buyers. For much of the day he bought American Express at a loss.

The specialist in Minnesota Mining and Manufacturing stock opened at $64 a share, down $6.75 from Friday's close. This was the biggest opening drop he had ever set. But it was not enough. Minnesota Mining closed on Black Monday at $51.

The size of some of the gaps between closing prices on Friday and opening prices on Monday raised serious concerns.

The regulating agencies looked closely at what the specialists were doing. Eastman Kodak fell 15 percent at the opening, and the specialist purchased more than 130,000 shares. The Coca-Cola specialist purchased 88,000 shares, and the stock dropped nine percent. Seven major stocks opened at prices at least ten percent below Friday's close. But by noon their prices had rebounded significantly.

"Openings involving such large price movements followed quickly by price recoveries should be scrutinized by the New York Stock Exchange to assure that the specialist met his obligations to ensure a fair and orderly market," the SEC recommended. "The [SEC] has noted several instances of specialist performance in opening their stocks that raise questions about the specialists' maintenance of a fair and orderly market."

Is it possible that specialists were instrumental in causing the crash? By pricing their stocks too low in order to open trading, specialists may have fed panic selling. They may have created an impression that the market was crumbling. As selling accelerated, few buyers stepped forward. So specialists, mandated by exchange rules to keep the market going, bought heavily, accumulating more stocks than they could sell. Thus, most specialists became net buyers on Monday. Their accounts strained as never before, specialists purchased millions of dollars' worth of stocks that no one else wanted. The SEC surveyed specialist operations in 67 major stocks. On 50 of those stocks, specialists bought more than they sold. Their average net buy position per stock was $2.2 million.

A CRISIS IN LIQUIDITY

To purchase such vast amounts of securities obviously requires tremendous sums of money. But the same panic that forced specialists into unprecedented buying turned off the money lenders. They closed their credit spigots, plunging specialists into a liquidity crisis.

In its investigation of the crash, the Presidential Task Force said some specialists may have lost all their cash and credit attempting to stabilize trading in their assigned stocks during the first minutes of Black Monday.

"The limited nature of some specialists' contributions to price stability may have been due to the exhaustion of their purchasing power following attempts to stabilize markets at the open on October 19," the Presidential commission said.

Reviewing the activity a month later, *The Wall Street Journal* in a report that won a Pulitzer prize said that one of the largest specialist firms ended the day with $60 million in stocks, three times its normal inventory. Trading rules require that purchases be paid for within five business days. But in this case, the specialist's bank refused to make any commitment when the specialist requested a $30-million loan in a series of telephone calls during the night, *The Wall Street Journal* said.

Another specialist, also turned down by his bank, was forced to merge with a well-capitalized brokerage house in a deal consummated at 3 A.M.

Dazed by the magnitude of Monday's plunge, banks were withholding credit from their best customers on Wall Street. The Big Board faced a tremendous liquidity crisis, one of the worst things that can happen to any capital market. Earlier loans to security houses were backed by stock, now vastly devalued, and banks were unwilling to extend their risks. But specialists were stretched to the breaking point. Specialists are supposed to bend against the winds, a buffer against the storm. But their financal resources were being exhausted. One estimate said that specialists lost two-thirds of their $3-billion buying power while trying to tame Monday's market.

Weeks later, the SEC noted: "Without the substantial specialist buying on October 19, it is highly likely that the market decline would have been even worse. Specialists often were the primary, and sometimes the only, buyers during the morning of October 19, and many were substantial buyers during the afternoon of October 19. Very little buying was effected by upstairs trading firms.... When the final wave of sell orders came late in the afternoon they [specialists] were incapable of stemming the subsequent decline."

In reconstructing the events of October, the Securities and Exchange Commission uncovered what it said were several instances of "questionable specialist activity":

- A number of stocks were opened at prices well below their Friday closings.

- When prices declined substantially, "a disturbing number" of specialists sold more securities than they purchased rather than buying to prop up orderly prices.

Moving ahead in our story, the SEC later said that specialist performance on Tuesday, the day after Black Monday, "was uniformly weak and reflected the panic and exhaustion prevelant on the New York Stock Exchange floor," and left lasting scars. Some specialists were absorbed by firms with more capital.

In its February 1988 report, the SEC's Division of Market Regulation said that specialists in the future may let stock prices rise or fall even farther before they enter the market because of diminished participation by upstairs firms and fear of sudden program orders. "Although more analysis should be done to test this assumption, the increased market volatility since October raises continuing concerns over liquidity in the market and the specialists' performance during volatile periods," the SEC wrote.

The Second Telephone Call

Specialists narrowly survived the 1987 crisis. But what might happen in another crash? On a sunny Friday in a future year, a man whom we will call Specialist Unlimited knew that the end was near for him. War had broken out in the Middle East, and on Wednesday the Dow had gone into one of its sharpest nosedives in history. The tabloid newspapers called it Wacky Wednesday.

By Thursday, the Dow had fallen so far that its losses exceeded the combined grand totals of the crashes of October 1929 and October 1987. Buyers vanished. Selling orders piled up. Investors were scared out of the market or were waiting to pick up bargains when prices approached the basement. So, doing his duty as a buyer of last resort, Specialist Unlimited had purchased millions of dollars worth of stocks during the unprecedented market collapse. His cash and credit line accounts were approaching zero.

Only a miracle could save him, but do miracles exist? Over the years, Specialist Unlimited had been reasonably attentive at Sunday church services. But he always felt uncomfortable when the preacher talked about miracles as if they actually had taken place. Specialist Unlimited thought of the Biblical miracles as symbolic teachings, not literal truths. Certainly he didn't expect water to be turned into cash on Wall Street.

Soon the opening bell would ring. If he could just keep his act together until noon, maybe, just maybe, the market would turn. Exchange officials had become so frightened by the unprecedented crash that they'd issued only one statement since Wacky Wednesday: "Due to heavy trading activity this week, the Exchange will close at noon on Friday to enable members to complete their paperwork."

By careful pricing at the opening and with a little more liquidity, Specialist Unlimited hoped that he could keep his stocks open and trading until noon. But he needed funds. He telephoned a banker, an old friend, to ask that his credit line be extended by another $1 million. Specialist Unlimited felt humiliated making the call. His family had been on Wall Street for several generations. He participated in civic activities that provided summer camps for kids from the Bronx and vocational training for high school dropouts. For years, he had served as treasurer of his church. His daughter had just written from her university that she was taking a course on how to apply skills of the hospitality industry in housing and feeding the homeless.

Specialist Unlimited and the banker were old family friends as had been their fathers and grandfathers. Although the banker had been a couple of years ahead of Specialist Unlimited, they'd both attended Yale. Two or three times a year they dined together at their club. On a couple of Saturdays each summer, Specialist Unlimited and his wife were invited to sail with the banker and his family off Long Island.

Perhaps this telephone call embarrasses him as much as it does me, Specialist Unlimited thought. After all, it's not his money. He is responsible to his board. Over the past two days, Specialist Unlimited had been forced to purchase about $4 million-worth of stock above what he could sell. Few buyers were attracted to his stocks. Again, the wealthy upstairs firms did nothing to help. But he tried to do his job and fulfill his responsibilities as a specialist, struggling in a plunging market to maintain orderly transactions in the stocks assigned to him by the Exchange.

The telephone was silent after Specialist Unlimited made his request. The banker was pausing. Specialist Unlimited's heart was pounding so loudly that he thought the banker could hear it at the other end of the line.

The banker was courteous while wording his reply in such a way as to discourage further conversation: "It has been a difficult week for all of us. I understand your position clearly, and I know how much thought *you gave to this matter before you called. I'm sorry my options are so narrow. Perhaps we can talk again in a few days." The call ended.*

Specialist Unlimited desperately needed cash before the market session opened. Failing to cover himself would mean instant bankruptcy. He could not wait a few days. So for himself and his firm, he knew that only one last honorable option remained. Quickly, to beat the opening bell, he dialed another number, also a close friend, and opened negotiations to sell the Wall Street firm founded by his grandfather, the gentleman in the oil portrait hanging above the office fireplace, a man Specialist Unlimited remembered only dimly from boyhood visits to a New Jersey estate. Great as his sorrow was in surrendering his legacy, he knew that passing his responsibilities to an organization better able to handle them was the right thing to do.

Not all specialists were so honorable. Some abandoned their responsibilities. Before the noon closing on Friday, several specialists on the New York floor and their counterparts in the Chicago futures pits, called the "locals" simply walked off the floor. Several pension funds, mutual funds and many individual investors suffered irreversible losses less than two hours after specialists handling their stocks disappeared, because nothing could trade. Prices started tumbling on a new downward spiral, crashing into the basement. Pensioners, aged men and women, were the ultimate victims.

10:30 A.M.: A SEMI-OPEN MARKET

By 10:30 A.M. on October 19, 11 of the 30 stocks listed in the Dow Jones Industrial Average still had not opened for trading, again because there were no buyers for the avalanche of sell orders. On a normal trading day, a sale is wrapped up in five minutes or less. But without buyers, no orderly market exists. Simply stated, no price can be found to conclude a transaction. Sales orders pile up. Specialists are helpless except to dip into their own funds and become the buyers of last resort. Also, when the stocks are not trading, price averages cannot be calculated accurately, and index figures are wrong or misleading. At 10:30 A.M., calculations were made on the few stocks that had opened for trading. Their prices indicated that the Dow Jones had dropped 94 points in the first 90 minutes of trading, but experts estimated that the plunge at that hour actually was closer to 200 points!

With that kind of error, 106 points, the market was worse than blind. It was totally wrong. Numbers were flying through the air, and no one believed them. The unprecedented volume of transactions delayed transmission of market statistics, essential to orderly trading. Market information became useless. With a number of key stocks not being traded, and delays in computer systems reporting sales, the compilation of accurate figures for the Dow Jones Industrial and the Standard & Poor's indexes became impossible.

Yet, wrong as they were, the Dow and other indexes continued to be posted. Indexes serve as road signs for stock traders, telling them when to buy and sell. And the indexes themselves are traded. Because of the state of Monday's market, wise players knew they could not trust the index numbers. But sales swept on at speeds faster than they could be recorded, causing index averages to become more and more faulty.

The worst possible thing that can happen to any capital market had occurred. The market was operating in the dark, without the price and sales-volume information on which investors base transactions. The price tags were obliterated, and no clerk could fill in the blanks.

11 A.M.: AT BEST, CONFUSION

By 11 A.M., volume on the New York Stock Exchange had reached an astounding 154 million shares, an all-time record for that hour in a trading day. But the market was wrapped in fog. Information systems were lagging hopelessly behind transactions. Screens and tickers were not reporting recent transactions, prices or volumes. The market's performance in the past hour and at the present time was as unknown and uncertain as its future.

"Until about 11 to 11:30 A.M.," the SEC reported, "the difficulty in obtaining firm stock prices and the resulting unreliability of index valuations made trading in the derivative markets chaotic at best."

Despite this confusion, market professionals assumed that a profit margin existed between indexes and actual stocks. On this assumption, a significant number of arbitrage programs were transacted through computers to capitalize on price differences between indexes and stocks, although the size of those price differences was being guessed at. The potential profit that could be earned in these arbitrage transactions was substantial. The Presidential Task Force estimated that one single transaction early in the day amounted to a return of 47 percent if calculated over one year. Similar opportunities to reap substantial profits developed throughout the crisis, on both Monday and Tuesday. The big-money guys played the arbitrage game with great vigor. Who said the crash was bad for everybody?

At the same time, while stock prices fell, many large institutional investors attempted to reduce their risks. Instead of using portfolio-insurance techniques, they started selling their shares rather than the indexes, because the floor seemed to be crumbling under the stocks. They had to sell before the value of their stock deteriorated beyond repair. The big investors, the large fund managers, saw the market tumbling, and they unleashed a flood of selling that overwhelmed everyone on Wall Street.

But there was some degree of order in all this madness. The selling wave was not as chaotic as it appeared. One of the authors of this book and two of his colleagues studied market performances during the crash. Their findings were published in the May-June 1988 issue of the *Harvard Business Review* in an article titled "The Smart Crash of 1987." They demonstrated that the pattern of sales throughout the crisis followed a rational line. Stocks of high-risk companies with weak corporate bases were sold more during the crash, and with greater price declines, than did the shares of fundamentally strong corporations. Bad as it was, there was some logic in the market crash. Surprisingly, and despite the collapse of the market mechanism, investors for the most part acted rationally during the crash.

NOON: PUSHING TOWARD DISASTER

The pace was accelerating. Like two huge rivers, stocks being sold by index arbitrageurs and portfolio insurers flowed into one gigantic system in the early afternoon. No dam could stop these churning markets. Strategists dealing in portfolio insurance were pumping massive sales into the market. During one 30-minute period, one program delivered a pair of sell orders containing two million shares each. From 11 to 11:50 A.M., more than 93 million shares were traded.

Arbitrage programs sold about seven million shares during the lunch hour. At the same time, nine million shares were sold in portfolio strategies. From 1 to 2 P.M., arbitrage and portfolio sales totaled approximately 19.7 million shares. The big-money guys were pushing the disaster to its limit. By selling in massive quantities, all of them attempted to desert the sinking boat at the same time.

"The most significant factors during the afternoon market downturn appear to have been the convergence of stock selling from index arbitrage and portfolio-insurance strategies around 1:30 to 2, and continued selling from portfolio-insurance strategies thereafter," the SEC said.

As we will see later, for the most part this wave of selling resulted from attempts to dismantle crippled portfolio insurance programs rather than from the continued use of computer programs as an investment strategy. At this point, it became clear that not much is insured by portfolio insurance when a crisis strikes.

1:09 P.M.: WILL THE MARKET CLOSE?

Sometimes a statement explaining what is not happening can cause a great deal of trouble. At this hour, the Dow Jones news wire flashed a report to Wall Street from David S. Ruder, who had been appointed chairman of the Securities and Exchange Commission just two months earlier. In Washington, Ruder said he had not discussed the possibility of a trading halt on the New York Stock Exchange with President Reagan or exchange officials. But Ruder also said that "anything is possible" and added that "there is some point, and I don't know what that point is, that I would be interested in talking to the New York Stock Exchange about a temporary, very temporary halt in trading."

This was a scary announcement, interpreted by some people on Wall Street to mean a trading suspension was in the works. If the market was going to close, traders could waste no time in selling off their portfolios. If they waited too long, and the market closed before they sold, their losses could run into the millions of dollars. Many of their stocks might be nearly worthless when the market reopened, whenever that might be. Several traders did not wait a moment. They dumped their shares to get out of the market as speedily as possible. The Presidential Task Force reported that between 1:15 and 2:05 P.M. the Dow Jones Industrial fell from 2,081 to 1,969 points, breaking through the 2,000-point barrier for the first time since January 7, nine months earlier. Futures indexes also plunged to frightening new lows.

By 1:25 P.M., the SEC announced that it was not discussing a closure of the stock market. But this word came too late. The damage was done. The Presidential Task Force gave this evaluation of the confusion created by SEC statements: "The uncertainty created by the possible inability to sell may have exacerbated the dramatic selling pressure. In fact, between 1:30 and 2 P.M. one portfolio insurer sold 1,762 contracts, worth $200 million. . . . In addition, during this same period, this portfolio insurer sold $500 million of stocks." Many arbitrageurs and other investors contributed to the avalanche of sales during this period.

2 P.M.: BLOOD ON THE STREET

A short-lived rally opened at 2:05 P.M. Why? Nobody knows. Perhaps the worse was over, and a turnaround had started. For a while that was the way it looked. The Dow rose approximately 50 points to the magic 2,000 level. Index futures also climbed significantly and actually led the rally, pulling up hundreds of stocks. At 2:34 P.M. the market looked good. An hour-and-a-half remained until closing, enough time to erase the nightmare. Traders were hoping for a happy end to a long and wrenching day. But their hopes were too good to be true. The Presidential Task Force estimates that most of the buying during this short revival was conducted by investors who were trying to cover losses suffered during earlier transactions. By 2:35 P.M., the rally had stopped.

Then another downward rout started. Only the closing bell at 4 P.M. halted this final plunge in prices. The large institutions still were selling. Commencing after 10:30 A.M., one major pension fund had sold 27.3 million shares scattered throughout the remainder of the day. Mutual funds, with stock investments in the billions of dollars, were bombarded with telephone calls from panicky investors who thought their mutual shares were evaporating. Fortunately, most funds keep enough cash on hand to pay off the weak at heart. But one major mutual fund complex sold 25.8 million shares to raise emergency cash. During the euphoric days before the crash, its policy was to keep its funds fully invested. Thus, it was forced to sell stocks in substantial quantities to generate cash to pay off redemption requests that had been rolling in since the weekend.

A smaller fund sold $7 million-worth of stock, about ten percent of its portfolio value. One mutual fund portfolio manager said the 30 percent he held in cash in August had dropped to zero by Monday as a result of paying off redemptions. To ensure cash flow, some funds borrowed against their bank credit lines. Another mutual fund tactic stunned investors who believed their shares could be cashed in immediately. Not so. Several funds discovered and applied a "small-print clause" that legally allows them to wait seven market days before honoring redemption requests. For the most part, this clause was exercised for the first time during the October crash. It came as a great surprise to most mutual fund owners, who had never read the obscure clause. Indeed, it was another unpleasant development of the day.

Fidelity Investments, which operates a 24-hour telephone service for its customers, increased the number of its switchboard operators by 20 percent over the weekend to handle 200,000 calls on Monday. On an average day Fidelity receives about 115,000 calls. With calls to some funds doubling over a normal day, several offices assigned executives to staff the phones. But many callers heard only a busy signal.

Not all mutual funds unloaded stocks. A number of them became net buyers on Black Monday, following a rule attributed to an early Rothschild: "When the streets of Paris are running with blood, I buy." Or in the words of Bernard Baruch, that grand old man of finance: "Buy when others are selling. Sell when they buy."

Indeed Wall Street did attract some buyers on Black Monday. The $5-billion Vanguard Windsor Fund purchased $120 million-worth of stock. But Vanguard's trader, Robert DiBraccio, had difficulty placing his orders with brokers. "The prices were moving so quickly that they [brokers] were afraid that taking five minutes to shop a block could mean they'd lose a point or more," DiBraccio said.

Greta Marshall, investment manager of the California Public Employees' Retirement System, gave orders to buy more than $30 million in stocks. "We always say we want to buy when other people are selling," she said.

Once on Black Monday, J. J. Jelincic, head trader for the California state fund, offered to buy a stock for what normally would be an outrageous bid: $2 below its last sale. Even bidding 25 cents under the last transaction is almost out of line in large transactions. Jelincic reported: "The guy said, 'That's brutal, but hang on.' He called me back 30 seconds later and said, 'You bought it.' "

Fortunately for the mutual funds, many investors telephoned to request that their investment be switched from stocks into money market accounts. Since mutuals manage both stock and money funds, customers could shift their accounts within one mutual family group rather than redeeming their shares for cash. Since 1979, investments in mutual funds had grown from $134.7 billion to $848 billion. Many individuals saw mutual funds as a better investment than anything offered by their neighborhood banks. Mutual funds had $539 billion invested in stocks and $309 billion in money market funds. These funds were replacing banks as major savings instruments. But, dangerously, they operate outside the banking regulations adopted by Congress as a result of the Great Depression.

3 P.M.: COMPUTER BREAKDOWNS

Transactions were being dumped into the New York Exchange's computer system, composed of about 200 Tandem minicomputers, in quantities never before handled. Computers executed more than 500,000 transactions. The previous daily peak was around 250,000. Through a typhoon of selling, information systems that normally flash market statistics promptly to traders were trailing hopelessly. Investors could only guess at prices and volume. During the afternoon, the New York Stock Exchange tape was running more than two hours behind. One trader said his screen showed the Dow Jones Industrial Average down by 178 points when the market closed. Actually, the Dow was 508 points down.

The unprecedented selling overwhelmed the mechanical printers that print out computer-delivered orders at trading posts on the stock exchange floor, creating significant delays in completing transactions. By noon on Black Monday, delays of 45 to 75 minutes had built up in the high-speed DOT system. Catherine Kinney, who oversees DOT, recalled later, "We started to throttle back traffic to the printers so we didn't blow it." The entire financial system could have collapsed because of failures in mechanical printers worth about $20,000.

On computer problems, the Presidential Task Force commented: "One major problem on the floor of the New York Stock Exchange was the breakdown of the computerized DOT system because of inadequate capacity. A total of 396 million shares were routed through DOT, but 112 million shares were not executed, of which 92 million were limit orders [orders to buy or sell a security at a specific price or better]. Because timely information was scarce, investors did not know if their limit orders had been executed and therefore did not know to set new limits."

A stop-loss limit order is designed to protect investors and minimize their losses when prices fall. Many investors believed they were safe. When their stocks declined to a preset price, the shares would be sold.

But for many, the system did not protect them because of computer delays in handling their orders. Numerous investors, particularly small ones, did not hear the bad news that their declining shares were not sold until two or three days later. Telephone lines to brokers were clogged. If investors did get through to their brokers, chances were high that the brokers had lost track of the stock in the melee. But, in most cases, it was not the brokers' fault. When a machine gun fires, not all bullets hit the target, and orders were flying through the air at machine gun rapidity.

So great were the delays that the Associated Press, which sends closing stock prices to newspapers throughout the world, said it was unable to start transmitting Monday's data until 9:30 P.M.—five-and-a-half hours later than usual.

A PRINTER'S LIFE

A weak link in any computer system is a small desktop machine, the automatic printer. Printers are descendants of the typewriter, the machine that opened the doors of business to women in the days when hems reached to the floor and bodices to the neck. Automatic printers are the great-grandchildren of manual typewriters and the old Teletype machines that, in a more leisurely era, banged out telegrams and newspaper articles at the noise level of a boiler factory.

In London, on January 7, 1714, a patent was granted by Queen Anne to Henry Mill, an English engineer, for "an Artificial Machine or Method for the Impressing or Transcribing of Letters Singly or Progressively one after another, as in Writing, whereby all Writing whatever may be Engrossed in Paper or Parchment so Neat and Exact as not to be distinguished from Print."

From that concept came the business-machine industry.

In an automatic printer, instead of typewriter keys pounding against paper and a carriage traveling from right to left, a small matrix runs horizontally back and forth across the page, creating letters and numerals out of small dots. Inventors figured out a way to make the matrix print every other line while moving backwards. The old manual carriage return on a typewriter essentially was a nonproductive act. After typing a line, the secretary in her high-necked dress pulled a lever that hauled the rubber roller and the typing paper it held back to the right so a new line could be typed.

But in this day of highly innovative finance, we can't afford to lose a single motion. A lost second is a nonproductive second. As Ben Franklin could have told us, a second saved is a second earned. So computers print out a line left to right, then the next line right to left. Not a second is lost. Electronic signals travel at the speed of light, 186,000 miles per second. On a manual typewriter, a skilled secretary can type 60 words a minute. Electric typewriters add ten words or so to the typist's speed, and far less pounding is required to operate the keys. Many years ago, Teletype printers were designed to print 60 words a minute automatically, later improved to 75 words a minute. Then came the early electronic printers at 120 words a minute, then 1,200 words a minute. Later models operate much faster. DOT printers at the New York Stock Exchange pour out about 3,000 words a minute. Printers have been developed that generate 13,000 lines a minute.

But the printer remains a machine. It operates with moving parts. They jam. They stick. They break. They wear out. If nothing else, the ribbon fades. Computer supervisors were forced to slow the system on Black Monday to save the printers. In a future crash with even more tumultuous selling, a printer that costs a few thousand dollars could blow a gasket while the repairer is out to lunch. By the time the technician finishes a Big Mac, a trader could miss enough information to buy a billion Big Macs.

In its report, the Presidential Task Force said, "On Monday, orders for 396 million shares were entered into the New York Stock Exchange's DOT system. This unprecedented traffic at times overwhelmed the mechanical printers that print DOT orders at certain trading posts, resulting in significant delays in executing market orders and in entering limit orders. These delays meant that market orders were executed at prices often very different from those in effect when the orders were entered."

That's like trying to use last year's price tag to purchase this year's new car.

If the computerized DOT system breaks down during a bigger crash in the future, trading could be delayed by several hours, not just by one or two hours as on Black Monday. A lengthy halt in computerized transactions would leave money managers helpless. With the trading system idle, managers would be stuck with stocks on which prices were collapsing. They would be unable to sell and move into better investments. The market would lose its continuity, its liquidity. Millions of dollars would drain out of their portfolios with no pumps to replenish.

In a crisis situation, a lack of information generates rumors that translate into panic. Can a bottleneck in a mechanical printer create a financial black hole? It came dangerously close in October, 1987.

On Black Monday, 28 percent of orders went unexecuted. Computers could not handle the deluge. In an even bigger crash, many more could be lost. Most of these would be limit orders, placed in advance to protect an investor by selling stocks automatically when their prices tumble. Traders would be unable to unscramble the mess. Quite likely, they would stop operations rather than risk losses, confusion and mistakes caused by an unreliable computer system. As for the poor investors, they might be able to pick up a few extra dollars to cover their losses by doing odd typing jobs with reliable typewriters.

4 P.M.: REAGAN: "THE ECONOMY REMAINS STRONG"

On Wall Street, the flood of selling roared through the afternoon. Trading in the closing minutes was extraordinarily heavy. Through the final 30 minutes, 63 million shares changed hands—35,000 shares per second pouring through exchange computers while prices tumbled crazily. The stock market had created its greatest debacle in history.

"The best thing that happened in the market today was the closing bell," one broker said. The Dow Jones Industrial Average had plunged an unprecedented 508 points, losing 23 percent of its value in six-and-a-half hours. An unheard-of total of 604 million shares, representing ownership of corporations large and small, passed from one owner to another. Prices on futures contracts declined 29 percent on a volume of 162,000 contracts. Every statistic that measured Monday's frenzied activities set a new record.

Earlier this year, Japanese investors, awash with cash, bought heavily in U.S. stocks, providing significant support to the New York market. But, growing wary of the declining value of the U.S. dollar, Japanese buying vanished on Monday like a ninja warrior. But surprisingly, the evidence shows that on this critical day Japanese investors sold very few shares from their large U.S. portfolios even though the market was decimating the value of their holdings.

Call it the Ginza syndrome. Japanese investors pay close attention to the asset value of a stock rather than what it earns in dividends. They consider what a corporation will be worth if it liquidates. They know that the price of one inch of land on the Ginza, Tokyo's main shopping district, is astronomical.

In business, politics and family relations, the Japanese are among the most conservative people in the world. They plan every move in excruciating detail. In the 1960s, the *Mainichi Shimbun*, one of Japan's largest newspapers, spent more than two years planning a one-day move of its offices a distance of about one mile, from a pre-World War II building to the new Palaceside Building overlooking Emperor Hirohito's Imperial Palace. Calculating every step, precise times were computed right down to the second that each piece of furniture and equipment would be moved from the old office, placed in a truck, driven to the new building, unloaded and set down on the exact spot that had been marked on floor plans months earlier. The move went like clockwork because nothing unforeseen occurred.

Oftentimes, Japanese find it difficult to adjust their carefully constructed plans if something unexpected happens. Some historians believe that Japan might have prolonged the Pacific War, perhaps even winning some territory in a final settlement, if the Imperial Navy had followed its successful attack against Pearl Harbor by immediately sending its bombers back to Hawaii and on to California. Instead, despite its almost-fatal and unexpected blow to the U.S. Navy at Pearl Harbor, Japan withdrew in accordance with its original battle plan. And so, throughout the surprise developments on Black Monday, most Japanese investors remained on the sidelines, retaining their shares in corporate America, neither selling nor buying.

The bulk of foreign selling came from European investors. Stock sales by foreign investors are difficult to isolate from the grand total because much of their activity is settled through U.S. banks. But experts identified at least four major sell programs totalling over nine million shares that were funneled through foreign banks.

Foreign ownership of American stocks should not be overemphasized. At the end of August, foreigners held about $200 billion in U.S. securities, only seven percent of all U.S. equities. Western Europeans owned the most, 60 percent; followed by Canadians, 16 percent; and Japanese, seven percent.

While the market rolled down the mountainside, Treasury Secretary Baker was meeting with West German finance officials. He had left Washington on Sunday to visit Sweden, Belgium and Denmark. But the Wall Street crash cut short his scheduled one-week trip. He stopped at a Frankfurt airport hotel to meet for three hours with German Finance Minister Gerhard Stoltenberg and the president of Bundesbank, Karl Otto Pohl, the nation's central banker. After four days of criticizing Germany for allowing interest rates to climb, Baker issued a statement following the airport session and said that he and the Germans "agreed to continue economic cooperation. . . including cooperation on exchange-rate stability and monetary policies." But for world markets, the pledge was late.

THE NIXON *SHOCKUS*

Given Baker's previous record, he performed rather well with the stubborn Germans. He moved away from damaging statements that he had made to the press several hundred Dow Jones points earlier. But what if Washington took the shackles off the dollar and let it float in the open market to find its own value? It happened before.

In Japan, they call several surprise statements, issued in 1971, the Nixon *Shockus*, referring to unexpected announcements that were made from Washington during the Richard Nixon–Henry Kissinger years. They became *shockus* because the White House neglected to discuss its decisions with Tokyo in advance although they deeply affected Japan's foreign and domestic fiscal policies.

Before making these announcements, Washington even ignored its embassy in Tokyo. American diplomats based in Japan sometimes got their first word on basic U.S. policies by listening to newscasts that are broadcast on the hour, every hour, by the U.S. Armed Forces Radio network that operates overseas to entertain and inform American troops.

Nixon delivered his biggest *shocku* to the Japanese when he suddenly announced that the United States was going off the gold standard. This would permit the dollar to float in terms of other currencies and, at least in theory, find its own value by supply-and-demand forces in international trade. Overnight, the value of the Japanese yen in terms of U.S. dollars increased, making Japanese exports more costly in America. Nixon took this step without consulting with or notifying Japan. Even Herbert Stein, the economist who served under Nixon as chairman of the Council of Economic Advisers, wrote in his book, *Presidential Economics:* "Who would have expected Richard Nixon. . . to go off the gold standard and to float the dollar?"

Another *shocku*, announced just as unexpectedly, altered one of the basic planks in America's foreign policy in the Far East. Since World War II, the United States had courted Japan assiduously to support Washington's foreign policy. For the most part, Tokyo did. But, without so much as an advance telephone call to Japan's Ministry of Foreign Affairs, Nixon shifted America's long-standing China policy that for years had appeared to be carved in stone. The White House announced that President Nixon was going to visit the Chinese Communist leaders in Beijing—a government that America up to that time had considered to be illegitimate. What's more, Washington said, Dr. Kissinger already has completed a secret trip to China. Nixon's meeting with Chairman Mao Tse-tung led the United States to establish formal diplomatic relations with Beijing and derecognize America's World War II comrade-in-arms, Generalissimo Chiang Kai-shek.

A year or so after those two *shockus*, a U.S. ambassador was sitting for a haircut in the American embassy in Tokyo (once known as "Hoover's folly" because of the high costs of building the embassy during the Great Depression) when his radio (made in Japan) announced that Washington would issue an important announcement within a few hours. Fearing another *shocku* on which he had received no advance word, the ambassador immediately got on the telephone to Washington, where it was night. The only person he could reach was the wife of a high State Department official. She said that she didn't have a clue what her husband was planning. As it turned out, the ambassador could breathe easily. This time, the *shocku* concerned the Middle East.

A New Shocku
In a year yet to come, the night duty officer in Japan's Ministry of Foreign Affairs is sitting in his office with his radio (also made in Japan) tuned to NHK, the Japan Broadcasting Corporation. He is a graduate of the elite Tokyo University. His diploma virtually assures him that he will become at least a bureau director in the Foreign Ministry before he retires. He's listening to an NHK correspondent based in Washington read the news.

"The secretary of the Treasury announced today that she will urge Congress to restrict trading by foreigners in American stock markets. The securities industry in the United States has argued that foreign investors

*own such a high percentage of American stocks that they can manipulate
the market for the sole benefit of their own economies at home."*

*As Japanese do, the night duty officer inhales, making a hissing
sound. "A new shocku!" It does not occur to him to consider how for
several decades a cheap and undervalued yen had helped Japan become one of the world's wealthiest trading nations.*

*At dawn, key economic officials are called back to the Foreign
Ministry for an emergency meeting to work out a recommendation to
the Finance Ministry. This new shocku involves both diplomatic and
financial relations with the United States. Congress could wreck the
Tokyo-Washington alliance that has been so carefully nurtured by the
two governments over many years. Japan controls several billion dollars' worth of American securities. After three hours of discussions,
Foreign Ministry officials reach a consensus in a nation that makes all
decisions by consensus. They agree that Japan has no choice but to
pull out of the U.S. capital market immediately, right now, even
while night is falling on New York.*

*Washington's new restrictions could freeze Japanese funds, per-
haps impose new taxes and God knows what other new shockus the
Americans might be cooking. Despite generally friendly relations
with Americans, Japanese still remember the Hiroshima and Naga-
saki atomic bombs and tend to forget their surprise military attacks
against Russia in 1904 and the United States in 1941.*

*The time has come for Japan to take care of itself and turn back to
the yen—the currency of a nation where achieving consensus is a par-
amount way of life, where shockus are not acceptable. In Japan, you
do not keep your shoes on when you enter a house with floors of
straw mat tatami.*

THE PRESIDENT: "I DON'T KNOW"

President Reagan, for one, did not know what to make of Black
Monday. Bravely, the White House issued a statement declaring that
"the underlying economy remains sound."

The statement continued: "Employment is at the highest level
ever. Manufacturing output is up. The trade deficit, when adjusted
for changes in currencies, is steadily improving. And, as the chairman of the Federal Reserve has recently stated, there is no evidence
of a resurgence of inflation in the United States."

In London, Margaret Thatcher reacted with a similar response. The underlying economy is strong, the British prime minister said.

Like all prepared statements, the White House pronouncement put the situation into articulate words. Earlier, encountering reporters on the run, the president described the significance of Wall Street events in words that probably reflected the reaction of most Americans who could not be expected to possess expertise in the complexities of finance and economics. "I don't know" was the president's first answer to reporters.

Meanwhile, Democrats saw a different situation than the view described in the carefully crafted White House statement. Massachusetts Governor Michael S. Dukakis, who later became the 1988 Democratic candidate for president, blamed Wall Street's bursting bubble on Republican "borrow-and-spend" policies.

Did the White House statement that "the underlying economy remains sound" reassure Americans who measure the nation's economy by the balance in their checkbook rather than by the Dow Jones Industrial Average? Who knows? Perhaps the statement accomplished nothing.

Most Americans live on or near Main Street. They define the state of the economy in terms of their paycheck, mortgage, car payment, the cash-register total at the checkout line and the god-awful cost of trying to send a kid to college.

It Ain't the Stock Market
The scene is Jake's bar in a later year. Two construction workers are sitting on bar stools near the taps with a couple of draft beers in front of them.

"The president says we're on easy street?"

"How the hell does he know?"

"Well, he was saying it ain't as bad as the Dow Jones looks."

"Screw the Dow Jones. You can't eat it."

"Well, you look like you're doing OK."

"Oh, sure. You know my kid that had the operation a couple of months ago? Well, the insurance company's not paying it all. I got loaded with a big bill."

"Least you got a job."

"Where's it getting me? The union didn't get us a decent scale last time around, and it's going to get damn tight before the next negotiations."

"Well, you didn't lose any money on Wall Street."

"You're damn tootin' I didn't. All this stuff on TV about the crash sure doesn't bother me, because I ain't got any stocks. So the President comes along and says we're all in good shape. Well, maybe he is. But my wife's brother out on the farm says he can barely make his monthly payments, and the corn's so dried up by the drought this year that he wouldn't be surprised to see it pop right there on the stalk."

"Yeah, it is tough. I know."

"Those guys on Wall Street are for the birds. There they were talking about the market going up every day, and it kept going up and up, and everything was supposed to be pink and rosy. Then the market crashes. You want to know something? I'm just as poor today as I was last year, and the stock market ain't got nothing to do with it."

Unfortunately, he was wrong. Two weeks later, he found a pink notice in his pay envelope. It said: *"Because of unexpected suspensions of several construction projects, the company has no choice but to reduce its work force at this time. We regret this decision, but you will be among the first to be called back. We hope this will be soon."*

OUT TO LUNCH

In a collapsing market, blue-chip stocks might seem to offer the greatest strength and the safest haven for investors. But not so on Black Monday. Blue chips are stocks issued by the largest and best-established companies in the nation. On Monday, shares on the New York Stock Exchange, where blue chips are traded, were battered worse on a percentage basis than the less expensive and less prominent securities sold on the American Stock Exchange or in the over-the-counter market.

- The NYSE composite price index plunged 19.2 percent.
- The Amex's composite index lost only 12.7 percent.
- The NASDAQ's composite index of over-the-counter stocks, issued by smaller and less well-known companies, fell the least, 11.35 percent.

How can this phenomenon be explained?

The crash of Black Monday was fueled by the large financial institutions, the big-money guys who deal on the Big Board. Large institutional investors do not trade much on the American Stock Exchange, and they transact relatively little business on the over-the-counter market. Furthermore, while the New York Exchange and the Chicago futures market were shedding value at speeds that even the computers could hardly handle, it became increasingly difficult, often impossible, to execute transactions on the American and over-the-counter markets. A number of over-the-counter and American dealers defended themselves against losses simply by closing their offices or taking their phones off the hook. Out for lunch—all day.

On Black Monday, Peter Robinson, a retired architect in Key West, Florida, decided to cash in $65,000 in mutual funds for a down payment on a boat. He expected the money to be delivered within 24 hours. But he got a busy signal every time he dialed his fund's toll-free 800 number over the next three days. Robinson finally called a branch office. By that time, his fund had lost money. To make matters worse, the fund representative told Robinson that he could not get his money for seven days. Because managers expected many people to cash their mutual funds in the market panic, Robinson's fund put into operation the little-used clause (discussed earlier in this chapter) permitting seven business days to pass before redemption.

For many investors, trading by telephone became impossible because of constant busy signals or unanswered calls. The U.S. General Accounting Office gave this summary in its post-crash study prepared for Congress: "Market-makers generally said their phones were ringing off the hook on October 19 and that, given the staff on hand, it was impossible to answer all the incoming calls. One said his phones were lit up like Christmas trees all day long. " Brokers complained that they would go bankrupt if required to staff their offices regularly to handle the amount of business generated by the crisis.

The Presidential Task Force found from its postcrash investigation that "some market-makers ceased performing their function merely by not answering their telephones."

Two days after Monday's crash, Forbes magazine conducted its own test of market telephone services. During a 24-hour period, Forbes telephoned the toll-free numbers of ten mutual funds, dialing each office eight times. Of the 80 calls, 24 went unanswered. At the same time, the magazine placed eight calls to five discount brokers. Thirty-six of the 40 calls hit a busy signal or went unanswered. One firm's 24-hour telephone number was busy repeatedly a week after the crash.

The North American Securities Administrators Association estimates that about 40 percent of the 50 million Americans who own stock earn less than $25,000 a year. In November, the Association opened a hot line for investors with complaints about how they were treated during the crash. In the first month, about 6,700 investors telephoned with 2,562 specific complaints. October losses reported by these callers totaled $57 million, with individual losses ranging from $62 to $5 million. Hot-line operators received numerous calls from investors who said they had lost their life savings, which had been accumulated for down payments on houses, retirement funds and money for their children's education.

Possible irregularities were reported. One woman said she lost her $250,000 retirement savings because she followed her broker's advice on a "foolproof" investment scheme. Another woman said her broker put her into an options strategy without first seeking her approval. She lost $30,000. A railroad engineer said he lost $150,000 and owed his broker another $300,000 because he was not provided adequate opportunity to satisfy a margin call (a broker's request during a down market to provide more security on a loan being used to finance a stock transaction).

FINALLY, THE YUPPIES SEE A BEAR MARKET

As the stock market fell, cash surged into U.S. Treasury securities. Investors were seeking a safe haven for the money derived from their stock sales. One estimate said that trading by big dealers in government securities increased by $58 billion over the norm to a daily average of $173 billion during the week. This rush of money into Treasuries caused their yield rates to fall and their prices to climb. The yield on Treasury bills, securities that mature in a year or less, dropped by one-half of a percentage point. Yields paid on long-term Treasury bonds also declined as their prices rose. One cause of the crash was the sharp increase in Treasury bond yields before Monday. The decline in Treasuries on Monday was significant.

That was Black Monday. At 4 P.M., the Dow Jones Average closed at 1,738, its lowest level in 18 months, since April 7, 1986. Easy come, easy go. The market euphoria vanished like fog in the morning sun. Less than a year later, 16,000 people had lost their jobs on Wall Street, and thousands of MBA finance yuppies were questioning whether they had selected the right career. Finally, they had seen a bear market.

The price of stocks listed on the Dow Jones Average had plunged by 23 percent in one trading day. That was the same percentage drop that occurred over two days in October 1929, threshold of the Great Depression. The signs were bad. In its investigation into the crash, the General Accounting Office said of Black Monday: "Had the precipitous decline continued for even one day, massive disruptions to the United States financial system might have occurred."

Had the collapse ended? At the close of Monday's trading, specialists on the New York Stock Exchange were carrying approximately $1.3 billion in unsold stocks, up from $900 million on the previous Friday. The Presidential Task Force determined that "this heavy inventory was a major factor in their [the specialists'] inability to make orderly markets the following day."

Could Tuesday be worse than Monday? Monday's record decline in stock prices caused the greatest loss in Wall Street's history. But Tuesday developed even greater disasters that rocked the very foundation of the system. Before Tuesday ended, the entire capital market came close to collapse. Tuesday's aftershocks were worse than Monday's earthquake.

6:30 P.M.: FROM DALLAS, A TELEPHONE CALL

In Dallas on Black Monday, Alan Greenspan, chairman of the Federal Reserve Board, was attending the convention of the American Bankers Association. About 6:30 P.M., he telephoned Washington from the Adolphus Hotel and talked with the Fed's vice chairman, Manuel Johnson. They exchanged several other calls during the night, discussing a course of action to meet Wall Street's financial crisis. Bankers were rejecting pleas from market specialists for more credit to see them through another day. Strapped for cash on Monday, specialists faced ruin unless they could get their hands on more money. They needed liquidity to continue operations. But bankers feared heavy losses from loans already secured by stocks, and they were in no mood to dive deeper. On Tuesday, Greenspan would move to center stage.

7

Tuesday, October 20

THE PREDAWN HOURS: A CHURCH LOSES ITS MONEY

The trading day ends in Asia and commences in Europe before U.S. markets open. And this trading day, the worst in Wall Street's history, carried the financial system to the brink of disaster.

On Tuesday, while America slept, one of the most radical reactions to Black Monday occurred in Hong Kong, where pirates of the South China Sea once operated and illiterates became millionaires. Hong Kong, with an area of only 391 square miles, is home for six million Chinese, many of them refugees who fled from next-door China after the 1949 Communist victory. For decades, Hong Kong was a sleepy port, serving as an entrepot in the world's trade with China. After World War II, it developed into one of the freest and most robust economies on earth. It's paradise for business.

Taxes are low, no more than 15 and 16 percent on individual and corporate income. Currencies trade freely. Vast sums of money move in and out of the colony without restrictions. No traces are left as to where the millions came from or to where they went. Noninterference in business is the government's rule, and most Chinese are too busy making money to fret over the colony's lack of an elected government.

It is said that Hong Kong contains more Rolls Royces per square mile than any other city in the world except London. Its urban population density, 24 times greater than New York, exceeds any other city in the world: 270,750 souls per square mile, packed into blocks of towering apartment houses that cling to steep hills. Only the super-rich live in houses. Mercedes-Benz sedans serve as taxicabs. Chinese entrepreneurs and their ladies wear the finest tailored woolens and silks, and display priceless jades in their mansions overlooking Fragrant Harbor. Peasants live in shanties built from packing boxes. Where but in Hong Kong would a developer build a highrise apartment house and tear it down before its first occupant moved in? That's exactly what he did the minute he obtained title to an adjoining tract that allowed him to erect an office building and earn higher rents.

Nothing seems improbable in Hong Kong. Not too many years ago, market manipulators were known to float rumors in the morning (Chairman Mao Tse-tung is critically ill in Beijing), deny the rumors in the afternoon and collect their profits before dinner.

St. John's Cathedral is the seat of the Anglican faith in Hong Kong and a pillar of the British colonial establishment. The nineteenth-century white, Gothic cathedral is located just below Government House, where the British governor lives, the island's center of political power. From the front portal of St. John's you can see the Union Jack flying proudly atop Government House, even on Sundays.

But, gradually, the British colonial presence is giving way to the Middle Kingdom. Chinese priests are being added to the cathedral's roster of British clergy. One Sunday service in the Mandarin language was scheduled to augment the English prayer book after China and Britain agreed in 1985 that the territory would be returned to Chinese rule on July 1, 1997.

Supported by wealthy British and Chinese, the cathedral is one of the richest churches in non-Christian Asia. It spent more than U.S.$70,000 fixing up an apartment for a new dean just a few months before Black Monday. For years, cathedral administrators have shared the Chinese passion for investing in the loosely controlled and often highly volatile Hong Kong Stock Exchange, sometimes viewed as little more than a gambling casino. Amahs and tycoons alike try their luck. So did the cathedral. The house of God lost a bundle when the highly inflated Hong Kong market collapsed in the 1970s. But the cathedral came back for another spin only to lose another bundle this October.

ARREST OF THE EXCHANGE CHAIRMAN

On Tuesday, officials of the Hong Kong Stock Exchange responded to their 11 percent loss on Black Monday with an action unparalleled in any other world market. They closed the exchange, and announced that it would remain closed for four trading days, until the following Monday. No one could have guessed the dramatic results. In less than one year, eight officials of the exchange, including its chairman, would be arrested on various corruption charges.

The Hong Kong Exchange claims more stockbroker members than New York, Tokyo or London. Chinese in Hong Kong love to gamble—on horses, mah-jongg and the markets. They gambled heavily when they suspended trading. With world markets in turmoil, Hong Kong investors lost flexibility to profit or protect their interests. By shutting down the securities market, they risked Hong Kong's efforts to become a trusted international financial center.

The chairman of the exchange, Ronald Li, 57, explained his action by telling reporters that Hong Kong needed time. "I hope that by the time we meet again, the world markets will be stabilized," he said. But for Li, the trouble had only started.

During a news conference to explain the closure, Li attempted to jail an Australian reporter for *The Sydney Morning Herald*. It happened this way.

Reporter.   Have you gone against your own collective rules by shutting down the exchange?

Li.   I resent your statement. I'm going to have you arrested.

A shouting match followed. No police were present. But the reporter left when Li ordered a couple of exchange employees to escort the Australian out of the building.

Newspeople present said that Li, obviously suffering from market shock, seemed to interpret the reporter's question, not as a query, but as a statement accusing the stock exchange of illegal actions. The reporter's question soon became the least of his worries.

Three months later Li was arrested by the Hong Kong government's Independent Commission Against Corruption. Seven other exchange officials were arrested in 1988 by the same commission, a suprainvestigative organ with wide powers to ferret out corruption in public and private life.

They were accused of accepting beneficial interests in shares of companies floating new issues on the exchange. Charges against the former stock exchange officials were pending in court when this book was written. A new slate of officials replaced them in the exchange.

Despite the trouble that Li and his colleagues later found themselves in, the decision at the time to suspend stock transactions seemed reasonable to Hong Kong's taipans and their bankers.

"It's a sound, sensible and brave thing to do," said Simon Keswick, chairman of Jardine Matheson Holdings, one of Hong Kong's oldest trading houses. "When there is a hurricane, close the door."

John MacKenzie of Standard Chartered Bank and chairman of the Hong Kong Association of Banks: "Unprecedented developments require that unprecedented action be considered."

But critics argued that Hong Kong's image as a free economy with unlimited access was tarnished when stock market officials unilaterally closed down operations. "This is not a stock market. This is a badly run casino," said Marc Faber, head of the Hong Kong office of Drexel Burnham Lambert of New York.

William Purves, chairman of the British-owned Hong Kong and Shanghai Banking Corporation, the closest thing to a central bank in the colony, said there was "no point in pretending that Hong Kong's reputation as an international financial center has not suffered."

Sir David Wilson, the British-appointed governor of Hong Kong, found himself in an embarrassing position. When the exchange closed, he was in the United States promoting Hong Kong as a free trade center. Earlier in October, even Chairman Li had visited New York to encourage Wall Street investment in Hong Kong.

The Hong Kong market had hoped to prevent further losses by closing for a few days. But when the exchange opened the following week, the Hang Seng Index plunged another 1,120 points, a drop of 33 percent.

ADVICE FROM THE EXCHEQUER

In Japan, the president of the Tokyo Stock Exchange made a bold move to draw buyers back into his battered market. Michio Takeuchi, the exchange's chief, announced that he would increase from 30 to 50 percent the portion of a stock transaction that could be financed with a loan. But prices on the Tokyo Exchange continued their perilous plunge on Tuesday, falling 14.9 percent during the day, the largest decline in 34 years. Only seven stocks increased in price compared with 753 that lost.

In London, the chancellor of the exchequer, Nigel Lawson, tried to calm his fellow citizens. "My advice to small investors is to remain calm," he said. "There is absolutely no reason not to do so." Britain's strong economic growth should "Hearten all Englishmen," Lawson said. While institutions were dumping stocks in New York, much of the selling in London appeared to be by individual shareholders. The policy of Margaret Thatcher's government to sell state-owned enterprises to the public had tripled the number of shareholders in Britain since 1979 to nine million. But brave words from the exchequer did not stem the hemorrhage in the City, London's financial district. Relentless selling continued. The *Financial Times* index of 100 shares fell 250.70 points, a fall of 12.26 percent, slightly more than Monday's record decline. In two days, the London market had lost 23 percent of its value.

Increasingly, investors are watching stock markets in other countries and for good reason. Investors are reaching across the seas to find good buys. The United States has been the major beneficiary in international trading. In 1986, foreign investors bought and sold $277.6 billion-worth of stock on U.S. markets, a record figure at that time. In the same year, American activity in foreign markets totaled only $102 billion, although that too was a record. About 500 corporations, based in several nations, truly are international. Their stock is listed on all major world exchanges. Dow Chemical and Citicorp, for example, have been listed on the Tokyo Stock Exchange since 1973, and IBM since 1974.

8 A.M.: A SERGEANT ON WALL STREET

Around 6:30 A.M. in New York City, John J. Phelan, Jr., chairman of the New York Stock Exchange, left his Manhattan apartment for his usual office breakfast with key members. He had asked for their analysis of Monday's market collapse. Apparently most of them believed that the outlook was reasonably good. Phelan, 56, had been a Marine sergeant in Korea—duty that would toughen any man— and he had worked on Wall Street since he was 24 years old. His job as chairman of the Big Board paid about $750,000 a year. Certainly his salary was well earned during the crisis.

Soft-spoken and cool-headed, Phelan started working with his father on Wall Street after graduating from Adelphi University in Garden City, New York. At age 31, he was appointed managing director of Phelan and Company, working on the trading floor that is the heart of the New York Stock Exchange. In 1975, he became a vice chairman of the exchange. In that post, he played an instrumental part in bringing computers into the exchange, a $200-million project that permits today's huge volume of trading that would have been impossible during his early years on the Street.

Both on and off Wall Street, Phelan has been a high achiever. He has served as chairman of the board of trustees of Adelphi University; a member of the board of advisors of the Center for Banking Law Studies at Boston University; and a member of the board of directors of Tulane University and the New York Medical College. He served on the Cardinal's Commission of Laity for the Archdiocese of New York. For his civic and church work, Phelan had received a number of awards that included the Knight Sovereign of the Order of Malta, Knight Sovereign of the Order of the Holy Sepulchre, the Wall Street Man of the Year Award from B'nai B'rith Youth Services, the Stephen S. Wise award from the American Jewish Congress and the Good Scout Award from the New York councils of Boy Scouts.

Today the former Marine sergeant faced one of his most critical decisions: whether to retreat and suspend trading on the New York Exchange or charge ahead. Wall Street was tense as the opening of the day's trading approached. "People walked into their offices at 8 A.M. thinking they were about to be skewered," said Jack Rubinstein, a broker at Bear, Stearns.

SAVED BY THE FED

In some nations of the world, particularly in underdeveloped countries, governments use a simple system to finance their operations when tax revenues and international loans are insufficient. They print more money. But turning a central bank into a printing plant can ignite runaway inflation. In the United States, the supply of money is controlled by the Federal Reserve System, the nation's central bank. The Fed, as it is called, controls money supplies in a more elegant way than by revving up the printing presses. In general, the Fed employs three major controls over the amount of money available to the nation:

- By purchasing bonds from the Treasury Department. To pay for these purchases, the Fed actually creates new money, thus increasing the nation's money supply.
- By selling Treasury bonds. This takes money out of circulation and into the Fed's vaults.
- By altering the discount rate. The discount rate is the interest rate that the Federal Reserve system charges its member banks for loans. A low discount rate means that banks can borrow money cheaply from the Fed. Depending on their needs, member banks decide whether to borrow from the Fed or not. If they do borrow, the banks, in effect, are increasing the amount of money in circulation. On the other hand, when the discount rate goes up, loans from the Fed become more expensive. Banks then are less likely to borrow, or they borrow in smaller amounts. The growth rate of the money supply then declines.

Before the crash, the Fed was selling bonds. Then, on September 4, the central bank increased its discount rate from $5\frac{1}{2}$ to six percent. These actions slowed the rate of money growth in the United States. In August and September the U.S. money supply was growing at an annual rate of 4.2 percent. But in the preceding 12 months, growth of available money had been running at 9.8 percent a year. Using its monetary tools, the Fed succeeded in cutting the money growth rate by more than one-half, indeed a substantial reduction.

Constrictions on money supplies increase the cost of borrowing that money, whether you are a bank, a business or a credit-card shopper. Banks increased their interest rates because it was costing them more to borrow from the Fed. From August 11 to October 19, the prime rate went up sharply, from $8\frac{1}{4}$ to $9\frac{3}{4}$ percent. The prime, a bank's heartbeat, is the interest rate that banks charge in loaning money to their best customers. An increase in the prime triggers a chain reaction. Interest climbs on business loans, credit cards, home mortgages, auto loans and other forms of borrowing. The economy tends to slow, because businesses and consumers may pay more to finance purchases. At the same time, interest rates also were rising in

Japan and West Germany, two of the world's most important trading nations.

When the gap between interest rates and stock yields increases, and that was the case in October, investors are tempted to sell stocks and put the money into investments that capitalize on the higher interest rates—bonds, for example.

In its study of October 1987, the U.S. General Accounting Office reported that market participants believed that rising interest rates "may have played a major role" in creating the crash. Attracted by higher interest earnings from bonds, and fearing the negative impact of higher interest rates on ecomonic growth and corporate profitability, investors sold their stocks.

Tuesday dawned grim. Banks were refusing to grant additional credit to specialists and dealers, many of whom had all but exhausted their cash reserves in buying up Monday's flood of sell orders. The only collateral that dealers could offer were bloated stock portfolios that had shed much of their value in Monday's crash. *The Wall Street Journal* reported that one bank refused prompt delivery of $70 million in West German marks that it had sold to a securities firm, fearing delays in payment. Even Japanese banks were threatening to stop lending funds from their vast resources for stock transactions. But dealers and specialists sorely needed cash credit lines for Tuesday's trading.

Big Board Chairman Phelan discussed the credit crisis by telephone with E. Gerald Corrigan, president of the Federal Reserve Bank of New York. Alan Greenspan, chairman of the Federal Reserve Board, had been on the telephone from Dallas Monday night. Greenspan canceled a speech that he was scheduled to deliver to the American Bankers Association on Tuesday and rushed back to Washington.

In one sentence, he issued a historic statement, simple in its wording but profound in its significance:

"The Federal Reserve System, consistent with its responsibilities as the nation's central banker, affirmed today its readiness to serve as a source of liquidity to support the economic and financial systems."

That was the support that lending banks needed to resume issuing credit to sorely pressed stocks dealers. The Fed has reassured banks that funds were available for cash-thirsty stock dealers. As Phelan told *The Wall Street Journal*: "The banks would be kept liquid. The banks would make sure everyone else in the system would stay liquid."

So urgent was the need for credit on Wall Street that Corrigan and other Fed executives personally telephoned major banks to assure them of support. The credit crisis was ended.

9 A.M.: STOP THE COMPUTERS

Before the markets opened, the New York Stock Exchange took an extraordinary step. Exchange officials asked their members to stop using the DOT system, the computer-driven network that almost failed when hundreds of millions of shares poured through its system on Black Monday. The halt was ordered to ease pressure on the system. Also, some Exchange officials believed that the ability of computers to conduct transactions involving astronomical quantities of stock in seconds may have exacerbated price drops and magnified them into even greater declines on Monday. By putting DOT out of action, the exchange hoped that stability would return to the market. It was a quick fix that failed. Wall Street's most unstable day followed.

DOT is the heart of stock-index arbitrage. Sitting at computer screens, program traders read the future price of the Standard & Poor's stock index, and the current price of the 500 stocks that comprise that index. When instantaneous gaps develop between the index and its underlying stocks, program traders sell the expensive item and buy the cheaper one. That's what arbitrage means—buying in one market and selling at a higher price in another market.

Trading in stock-index futures as a hedge against a loss in the market value of stocks started in 1982 in Chicago, and grew spectacularly. About five million contracts in stock-index futures were transacted in 1982. By 1986 the volume had grown to over 25 million contracts. In the week before the October crash, transactions in Standard & Poor's futures index averaged 106,400 contracts a day. Stocks covered by those indexes were worth about $16 billion. But the actual stocks were not traded. Instead, indexes of their anticipated future prices were bought and sold. These indexes represent securities that were worth more than double the average dollar volume traded daily on the New York Stock Exchange in September.

The idea of buying and selling futures indexes led directly to program trading as a strategy that capitalizes on split-second differences between the price of stocks and the theoretical price of their futures.

Stock futures also enabled institutional investors, such as managers of pension and mutual funds, to protect the value of their securities without touching them. This is called portfolio insurance. The system trades in futures rather than stocks, using profits earned on futures to cover losses on stocks or vice versa. Big institutional investors leaned heavily on futures during three critical days in October. About 6.3 percent of futures traded on Friday, October 16, were linked to portfolio-insurance selling. That percentage increased to 16.7 on Black Monday and to 25.5 the following day. About 39.9 million shares of stocks were sold in portfolio insurance on Black Monday but only 10.5 million shares the next day.

One important advantage of trading in index futures relates to the costs of market transactions. Commissions on indexes are much less than on stocks. Morgan Stanley has demonstrated that it costs 13 times more to trade a $120-million portfolio in the stock market than in the index futures market.

During certain critical periods in October, both index arbitrageurs and portfolio insurers were selling stocks heavily. They accounted for between 30 and 68 percent of the total volume of New York trading transacted in Standard & Poor's 500 stocks, the cream of the market. Some critics called the arbitrageurs and insurance practitioners the villains who created Black Monday.

Did program trading cause the crash? Any large trading, whether by program or otherwise, can move the market. But critics of program trading say that computer systems can kick off a downward spiral that feeds on itself, growing larger and larger as the market falls. They explain it this way. In a plunging market when prices reach a pre-specified level, the computer automatically executes a sale of stocks worth hundreds of millions of dollars. Because the first sale depresses prices, the computer triggers another sale, pushing prices down even further. Then another sale is generated inside the computer, and when a lot of traders follow the same strategy, on and on it goes like a stone rolling down a mountain, gathering more stones until they cascade into a landslide.

Other experts disagree. They argue that computers are controlled by people who would adjust programs before they run the market to a disaster. Also, they contend that data systems on the exchange were unable to keep up with the runaway market. Information lagged far behind actual trading. Thus, program systems became useless because they require accurate price information swiftly delivered. If the true relationship between cash market prices and future prices cannot be determined, arbitrage trading fails. Under the panic conditions of Monday and Tuesday, simultaneous buying and selling of stocks—and that's what arbitrage is all about—became impossible most of the time.

John Phelan, chairman of the Big Board, explained that he curbed electronic trading in an effort to reduce the flood of sales by institutions.

"Program trading, when the market isn't at extremes, adds to liquidity and helps institutional investors," Phelan told *The Wall Street Journal*. "However, when the market is at extremes, program trading does add to volatility, and that has everyone worried."

He also said that "we wanted to make sure our system was clear so the public had direct access." But some traders saw another motive, arguing that the SEC and the stock exchange were looking for a way to explain Monday's crash without undermining confidence in the general economy. So program trading became their scapegoat and a target for a fast fix. We will say more about program trading. But before passing judgement, let's follow the day's events.

9:30 A.M.: EVEN DUPONT WAS LATE

The stock market in New York and the futures market in Chicago opened with significant price increases. Like an inverse mirror image, the opening on Tuesday reflected the exact opposite of Black Monday. On Monday, sellers flooded the market, and there were no buyers. On Tuesday, the market opened, and it was so overwhelmed with buyers that many stocks could not open. Again, the specialists could not cope with the imbalances between buyers and sellers.

Some stocks required more than an hour to open. At 10 A.M., 95 of the Standard & Poor's stocks still were not opened because of a surplus of buyers. By 10:30 A.M., 11 of the 30 stocks that make up the Dow Jones Industrial Average remained closed.

In one sense, a stock exchange is nothing more than an auction house in which shares are offered for sale to the highest bidder that can be found at the moment. On a normal market day, a buyer usually steps forward with a bid for every stock placed on sale. Trading runs smoothly. The price and number of shares contained in each transaction is printed out on the ticker tape and displayed on video screens.

The term "order imbalances" refers to a market condition in which sellers outnumber buyers, or vice versa. When the market opened on Black Monday, specialists faced large imbalances on the sell side. Everyone was trying to sell, and buyers were few and far between. A reverse situation developed on Tuesday, when the opening imbalance was created by an excess of buyers. Such imbalances upset the flow of transactions through the stock exchange, and unfilled orders to buy or sell pile up on trading counters. Also, stock indexes such as the Dow Jones and the Standard & Poor's, which serve as pricing guides to market participants, become unreliable if key stocks in those indexes are not being traded.

Throughout Monday and Tuesday, order imbalances caused critical delays and periodical halts in trading numerous stocks, including some of the blue-chip shares that make up the Dow Jones Industrial Average. When several blue chips were closed, the Dow Jones was reduced to a guessing game. A total of 2,257 stocks were listed on the New York Exchange in October. Only about 1,500 are traded actively on a daily basis. On Monday, 195 trading delays and halts occurred. On Tuesday, there were 280 delays or halts.

Dealing with this problem, the General Accounting Office said: "Faced with huge order imbalances, New York Stock Exchange specialists halted trading or delayed openings in many stocks, making it impossible at times to determine transactable prices in many securities."

Because of the fast-paced confusion, some participants made a clean break "to back away from their markets, fearing they would lose everything," the General Accounting Office reported.

In the first hour after the exchange opened on Tuesday, with trading picking up slowly, a remarkable recovery occurred. The Dow Jones Industrial Average suddenly zoomed upward by nearly 200 points. The bond market also had started strong, and bargain hunters were combing the ticker list for good buys left in Monday's shambles. Aggressive bulls also dominated the futures market. Buying pressure from the big-money guys pushed Standard & Poor's futures contracts up by ten percent right at the opening. Will Tuesday erase Monday? It sure looked like it shortly after the opening bell.

But not for long. The gain was short-lived. Around 10:30 A.M. prices started plunging again. Specialists and major brokerage houses sold heavily from their inventories, swollen by early-

Monday purchases. The buying power of specialists on the floor was strained. Banks were refusing to extend any more credit. Dealers had spent about $2 billion buying stocks no one else would take. That was their limit. Buyers quickly became scarce.

Just as speedily as its earlier advance developed, the market suddenly went into a free-fall and lost 27 percent between 10 A.M. and 12:15 P.M. It was a rerun of Black Monday. Of this period, the Presidential Task force said that "at its low the S&P 500 futures contract price implied a Dow level of about 1,400." But a fall to 1,400 would be catastrophic, far below Black Monday's disastrous closing at 1,738. Nevertheless, at this critical point some dominant institutional traders could see a future as bleak as 1,400. This latest plunge destroyed all semblance of an orderly market.

Merck opened at 9:46 A.M. to such a wave of selling that it was closed eight minutes later. After short-lived rallies, other major stocks closed during the morning, including Sears, Eastman Kodak, Philip Morris, 3M, Dow Chemical and USX. As late as 11:25 A.M., even venerable DuPont hadn't opened for the day. The New York Stock Exchange was in serious trouble, perhaps its worst in history. The exchange, heartbeat of the nation's economy, was moving towards a complete meltdown, far worse than Black Monday. Trading in scores of major stocks stumbled to a halt, restarted with a jerk, then died again. Trading in some stocks never started. Fears grew that Wall Street could not last out the day.

A CONTRADICTION: IT'S ONLY PAPER

Strangely, the crisis on Wall Street contradicted optimistic business forecasts elsewhere in the nation. Eastman Kodak stock dropped $27.75 a share, a 31 percent loss. But in Rochester, New York, corporate executives predicted excellent earnings. Demand was strong for film, chemicals and other Kodak products.

In America's foreign trade, the decline in the U.S. dollar promised better business for export-oriented firms. During the first eight months of 1987, foreign sales of U.S. products totaled $161.53 billion, a 13 percent increase over the same period in 1986. For example, Nordson Corporation of West Lake, Ohio, was exporting about half of the equipment it manufactures, devices that apply adhesives and coatings. William P. Madar, Nordson's president, predicted that profits would increase by 75 percent.

"Corporate profits are nothing short of sensational," said Allen Sinai, chief economist for Shearson Lehman Hutton. "We have a trend here, momentum that won't be eased."

Third-quarter profits being reported in October showed major gains in a wide range of industries, from computers to retailers. Yet the stock market was in turmoil, presaging to some people the preface to another depression.

Some capitalists seemed unconcerned about the market. Sam M. Walton, listed by *Forbes* magazine as the wealthiest American, calculated that his family's shares in Wal-Mart Stores lost $500 million in Monday's plunge.

He did not call it a black day. "It's paper anyway," he said. "It was paper when we started, and it's paper afterwards. As far as I'm concerned, we're focusing totally on the company doing well and taking care of our customers."

An Wang, the Chinese founder of Wang Laboratories, dismissed Wall Street's influence on his operations. "It doesn't bother me either way," he said. "As long as the company is doing well, what happened does not affect me at all. This is a stock that goes up and down. Nobody calls me when it goes up 1,000 points or down 1,000. It's quite a bit of money, but it's all on paper."

NOON: APPROACHING CHAOS

By noon, the Dow Jones average had fallen 11.4 percent, dipping down almost exactly to the same level at which it closed on Black Monday. Market pressure was so tremendous that new records on sales volumes were set again and again on the downward slide. One of the busiest 30 minutes in Wall Street's history occurred around noon today, and also one of the most confused. Individual stocks were closing, then reopening, then closing, ad infinitum. All traces of normal market operations vanished. The market approached chaos. For a while, Wall Street securities resembled numbered Ping-Pong balls bouncing around inside a revolving cylinder in a giant lottery draw: no pattern to their movements, and no way to forecast the winning numbers.

12:30 P.M.: RETREAT ON ALL FRONTS

By 12:30 P.M. the Dow had collapsed to about 1,700 points, approaching its lowest level since the traumatic day opened. Where will it stop? No one could guess. Some traders doubted that the market, with its erratic and unpredictable movements, would be able to stay open.

In Chicago, officials in the futures and options markets were worried. Trading on the New York Stock Exchange had broken down on many stocks contained in the Standard & Poor's indexes. Key blue-chip shares remained closed or were shut down after brief trading. It was the same story: Nervous investors were trying to sell millions of dollars' worth of stock that no one wanted to buy. Specialists were unable to maintain a continuous market. Wall Street was in such chaos that the information systems that track and record trading were providing misinformation. The stock indexes could not be believed. Without an adequate number of stocks being traded in New York, the indexes that averaged their prices in Chicago collapsed into hollow, meaningless shells with no value as trading instruments.

By any standard of an orderly market, midday Tuesday was the worst inning Wall Street had ever witnessed. And the chaos spread across the country to other financial markets.

Leo Melamed, chairman of the Chicago Mercantile Exchange, telephoned Big Board Chairman Phelan to discuss the breakdown. He heard more than he had expected. Phelan told the Mercantile chairman that directors of the New York Stock Exchange were meeting to decide whether to close the Big Board. If New York suspended stock trading, Melamed feared that the closure would precipitate massive selling of futures in Chicago before they became all-but-worthless, and exhaust the Mercantile's liquidity.

So he took the only step he could. At 11:15 A.M. (12:15 P.M. in New York) the Mercantile Exchange halted trading in Standard & Poor's 500 futures contracts. About 30 minutes earlier, the Chicago Board Options Exchange also had suspended dealings in the 500 index for the same reason that bothered the Mercantile: Too few stocks that comprise the index were trading in New York.

The retreat from futures swept across a broad front. In rapid order, trading in stock indexes was closed on the American Stock Exchange, the Pacific Exchange, the New York Futures Exchange and the Kansas City Board of Trade.

By now, Phelan truly was worried. He considered closing the New York Stock Exchange immediately, fearing that it might disintegrate into total chaos. Such an action would send violent shock waves through the U.S. and world economies. Although many complex factors contributed to the Great Depression of the 1930s, most people today mention only one explanation. In the minds of millions, history is simple: The stock market crashed in 1929, and as a result the Great Depression followed.

Wall Street is viewed as a barometer without peer. In the minds of many Americans, if the market shatters, then a chain reaction commences. Banks close, corporations fail, governments fall and dispossessed capitalists leap out of windows. The psychological damage is as great as the financial disaster. No one ever had closed the Big Board since November 1963, just after the assassination of President Kennedy, and even then it was just for a short time. And now markets were in retreat across the front, and ex-sergeant Phelan faced a grave decision.

Suddenly, a hopeful message was flashed. Karsten Mahlmann, chairman of the Chicago Board of Trade, was on the telephone to New York. He reported that his exchange still was trading future contracts on the little-used but highly reliable Major Market Index. Although traded infrequently, the MMI contains only the bluest of the blue chips: 20 of the largest and soundest corporations from among the 30 industrial companies that make up the Dow Jones index. But Mahlmann was worried. The signs were all wrong. The MMI was trading this morning at its biggest discount in history to the cash value of its index. When the American Exchange halted options trading, the MMI plunged even further. But a ray of hope remained. Although other markets were in disarray in New York and Chicago, the MMI was clinging to life, still breathing, although weakly. Perilous minutes ticked away, but 17 of the 20 MMI stocks still were being bought and sold. Then, in one of the most significant moves of the day, the Board of Trade made a decision that many analysts believe prevented a complete breakdown on Wall Street. The Board decided to continue trading the MMI; in effect, giving a crutch to the crippled system.

"We felt that we had to stay open to do our job, to provide liquidity," Mahlmann told *The Wall Street Journal*.

Markets were fast approaching their points of no return. Stocks and futures were twisted into a vicious net that could drag both markets into disaster. The Presidential Task Force explained the dangers this way: "The stock market 'drafted' down in the wake of the futures market. The result was sell-side order imbalances [more sellers than buyers] in both markets, leading to the near disintegration of market pricing." Heroic actions were demanded to prevent the crisis from wiping out all markets.

Big Board officials and floor directors representing specialists gathered in the chairman's office around noon. Pressures on them were tremendous and building up by the seconds. Value was draining rapidly out of huge stock portfolios that supported the nation's pension plans, insurance companies, mutual funds and other depositories of great wealth. Nearly all trading in futures and options had halted. Large investment houses were suggesting that the Big Board be shut down. The situation was so desperate that a plan was considered to seek $1 billion from Wall Street firms to prevent specialist firms from going bankrupt. If specialists failed, the market would vanish.

The very roots of capitalism seemed at stake. Was Karl Marx correct when he stated that capital can create no additional value? Was the stock market—where the value of capital ebbs and flows— doomed? Phelan said he talked with Howard Baker, the White House chief of staff, who urged him to remain open if at all possible.

Then it happened. In a period of about 20 minutes, starting around 12:30 P.M., the MMI staged the most remarkable rally in its history. Like a geyser on a sterile plain, at a moment when it was the only major index still being traded, the MMI suddenly gushed upwards by an extraordinary 90 points. The MMI's high-premium stocks make each of its points worth about five points on the Dow Jones Industrial Average. Thus, its swift recovery equaled a 450-point boom on the widely trusted Dow Jones, almost equal to Black Monday's plunge.

The Dow did not actually gain 450 points. But it climbed quickly by 126.2 points. The impact was positive, at least in a psychological way. But cautiously, the SEC said: "While the rise in the MMI may have had a psychological impact on stock prices, it appears to have had no direct effect on trading."

The Fed's pledge of credit support and the turn of the MMI pulled Wall Street away from the brink. The market's footing remained perilous, but a new course now was set.

Why did the MMI recovery so dramatically? How was it saved at the precise moment that the Big Board faced closure? Some evidence suggests that the index may have been manipulated deliberately in a supreme effort to restart a bull market. Concentrated buying of the MMI could force that index up with relative ease, because the general volume of MMI trading typically is low. Perhaps traders thought they saw bulls on the horizon and started buying. Perhaps a few major security firms executed a carefully crafted plan that was designed specifically to elevate the MMI.

Evidence to support the theory of intervention by a few giant firms can be seen in the nature of the trading. During the MMI rally, only 808 contracts were traded. About 70 percent of the contracts were purchased at low commission rates. In general, these rates are available only to major Wall Street firms. But, overall, the evidence is mixed and inconclusive.

Two reporters for *The Wall Street Journal*, James B. Stewart and Daniel Hertzberg, won a Pulitzer Prize, journalism's highest award, for their minute-by-minute analysis of Terrible Tuesday. Their lengthy article was published one month later on November 20. They started their account, a sterling example of financial writing, with this captivating paragraph: "A month ago today, the New York Stock Exchange died. But within an hour or two, it was raised from the dead."

Stewart and Hertzberg wrote that a burst of bullish sentiment may have sparked the MMI rally. But they continued: "Some knowledgeable traders have a different interpretation: They think that the MMI futures contract was deliberately manipulated by a few major firms as part of a desperate attempt to boost the Dow and save the markets."

Manipulation or not, clearly the big-money guys who had provided the impetus for Monday's market collapse reversed themselves and pushed the index upwards.

The MMI rally was encouraging, but problems remained. From 12:30 to 1:45 P.M., 145 stocks were not being traded in the New York Exchange. They were vital shares, representing 25 percent of the Standard & Poor's index.

1:45 P.M.: THE INSULTED EXECUTIVES

Then came another giant shot of vitamins. News was flashed that several major U.S. corporations had been or were planning to buy back their own stock. With security prices in the basement, corporations could sweep up their own shares at bargain prices. In doing so, management would help restore the confidence of stockholders and employees even though their companies had been devalued by Wall Street. In some cases, corporate workers, proud of their company and sensing a bargain, joined executives in purchasing their own devalued stocks.

Altogether on Monday and Tuesday, U.S. corporations announced that they were buying back approximately $6.2 billion of their own stock, the Presidential Task Force reported from its crash investigation.

Some corporate executives said they were personally insulted to see their stock collapse on the market, and they bought to save their pride. "My company was cut in half in terms of market value, and we take this very personally," Roger M. King told *The Wall Street Journal*. His family controls 40 percent of the shares in King World Productions, a syndicated television programming company.

William Roper, Jr., chief financial officer of a San Antonio computer-maintenance firm, said that when a corporation buys back its own stock "you are sending a signal to the market, to customers, to employees."

Elias Zinn, chairman of Entertainment Marketing, saw his company's stock fall on Tuesday from a recent $16.25 to $3.75. Fine. He said he would accept the low market price and purchase 500,000 shares ($1.8 million) in order to increase his 24.5 percent ownership of the company by about four percent. At the stock's earlier price, that transaction would have cost Zinn $8.1 million. For Zinn, a splendid bargain.

Out in Las Vegas, some employees of Circus Circus Enterprises, also bought their own stock. Naturally. They know a good gamble when they see it. They operate a casino hotel. Some corporations grabbed up their bargain-basement shares in order to place them into programs benefiting employees—including profit sharing, stock options and employee stock-ownership plans.

A significant point dealing with probable causes of the crash was made by an engineering consulting firm in Beaver, Pennsylvania. It is one of the nation's few publicly traded corporations in which most of the shares are owned by employees. Its stock fell only a quarter of a point on Black Monday, closing that day on the American Exchange at $8.25. Donald Baker, the company's treasurer, contended that its stock did not crash because the shares are owned by employees rather than institutional traders. He argued that the stocks that tumbled were the ones owned by big investors who sold on a massive scale. His shares were safe with small investors.

The number of corporations buying back their own stock was increasing a few days before Black Monday and accelerated greatly on Tuesday while the market scraped along near the bottom. By the end of the week, more than 100 companies had announced that they would repurchase their own stock. These deals included 20 million shares being bought back by USX Corporation, and 45 million shares by Ford Motor Company. Others were such giant organizations as Citicorp, General Motors, Chrysler, McGraw-Hill, IC Industries, IBM, Bristol-Myers, Allegis, MCA, Honeywell, ITT, Merrill Lynch, Shearson Lehman Hutton and four regional Bell holding companies. Many smaller companies followed suit.

"Around 2 P.M., the combined effect of buybacks already announced and those expected turned the equity market around," the Presidential Task Force on Market Mechanisms reported.

After all, some rationality prevailed in the system with greater effect than the possible manipulation of one futures index as some observers contend.

2 P.M.: A RETURN TO LIFE

Near 2 P.M. the market started another climb, bolstered by corporate and employee confidence in the health and future of their companies. "It looks like there's almost a get-together on the part of corporate America to prop up the market," said Stanley Abel, a consultant specializing in buybacks. "They wanted to make a demonstration of their confidence."

Orders to buy stock had started to accelerate shortly after 1 P.M. Reassured by the Federal Reserve that their cash requirements would be met, specialists and other firms were able to execute orders with confidence. During the week, Chemical Bank of New York increased its loans to security firms by $400 million above normal. At Bankers Trust, a spokesperson explained: "We were able to accommodate routinely the financing requirements of our major customers in an environment characterized by great uncertainty. The requirements of most others were met after greater-than-usual consideration."

The market was returning to life. Trading in Merck reopened at 1:15 P.M. IBM reopened at 1:26 P.M. At 2 P.M. USX reopened. All the stocks in the Major Market Index now were being traded. Phelan, the ex-sergeant, told other exchanges that the battle had been won, at least for the day. The New York Stock Exchange would not close. Trading in options and futures resumed.

By 3:30 P.M. the Dow had rocketed upward more than 160 points. It was the third recovery posted by the industrial average during a day marked by one crisis after another with financial fire fighters rushing in to save the system. In the last 30 minutes of trading, the closely watched Dow reversed its course, losing 75 points but remaining ahead of Black Monday.

The Cascade Scenario

In a future year, two money managers for a conservative investment fund are meeting to discuss the falling market.

"Listen. This decline won't last. The market's got strength. If we move fast, we can pick up some damn good bargains right now."

"Hold on. We're not speculators."

"What the hell do you mean? The market's safe. This correction in prices just happens to present us with excellent opportunities to pick up some large blocks that will appreciate before the week's over."

"Too dangerous now. Let's wait. We probably can buy much cheaper tomorrow."

The call of nature interrupted their discussion. Standing side by side in the men's room, one portfolio manager said: "Look, you may be right about those bargains. But I just can't risk buying anything right now. I got a kid starting in college next year, and I can't afford to lose this job. We better liquidate where we need it—hey, I don't mean that as a pun. Let's play it safe."

They did. They continued to sell baskets of stocks in program trading and move into U.S. Treasury bonds, a strategy with its own buzz word—asset allocation. But they could not always follow their computer's recommendations. Because of heavy selling, information feeding into stock indexes was lagging so far behind transactions as to make computer indications incorrect.

The cascade effect started, setting off a record decline in prices and, in the process, emasculating program insurance.

Here is how the cascade effect happens. The government announces negative news such as an imbalance in America's foreign trade that has reached an unexpected height. Investors know that this bad news will drive stock prices down.

Anticipating the decline, managers of investment funds tell their traders to start selling endangered stocks and to buy Treasury bills. Program traders move in to sell their futures indexes in an effort to protect their shares. This activity depresses prices on indexes. Then a price difference develops between futures indexes and the cash price of their underlying stocks. Arbitrageurs enter the picture, selling stocks and buying futures. This action pushes stock prices down even further. Then the entire process starts all over again, cascading the market into an even deeper downward spiral.

Prices decline rapidly. Information systems that track the market fall hopelessly behind, reporting prices that are far out-of-date. Dependent on accurate and current prices to execute portfolio insurance, institutional investors give up on protecting their stock and, returning to old-fashioned damage control, simply sell the stock straight. This pushes prices down again. A crash is underway.

Without accurate information, market-makers, in order to protect themselves in an uncertain and declining market, increase the spread between the prices for which they will buy and sell a stock. This interferes with market efficiency and discourages trading. A broker may share what little market information he or she possesses with colleagues, friends and a few favored clients. Others, largely small investors, are stranded in the dark. Rumors are created. Some rumors are planted to influence the market. Loss of confidence spreads. Chaos results.

4 P.M.: THE JOKES BEGIN

Like a yo-yo top, so named in the Tagalog language of the Philippines, the Dow Industrials rose and fell through three recoveries and three crashes. On Monday, the Dow Jones had fallen on a steady trajectory like an airplane gliding to a crash. But Tuesday's market went into wild gyrations, soaring to peaks and crashing into valleys. Its sharp fluctuations carried it from 26 points below Monday's closing to 200 points above, ending at 102.27 points ahead of Black Monday.

It was one of the most volatile days in Wall Street history. At one time or another, markets for futures and options fell, one by one, into complete disarray. Trading halted. Cash evaporated. Uncertainty reigned. The Big Board almost folded. If Monday was black, then Tuesday was treacherous, rife with trading systems that were collapsing, information systems that were wrong, and brokers who didn't know who they could believe or trust. Around noon on Tuesday, the entire American financial system was close to a complete meltdown.

The most skilled traders could have been impaled on one of the spikes formed by stock-trading graphs. Yet trading ended on the New York Stock Exchange with the Dow Jones standing at a reassuring level above its closing price on Black Monday. That was the largest recovery the Dow had ever posted in a single day, achieved just 24 hours after its greatest decline. Trading volume also set a new record: 613.7 million shares, nearly six million more than Monday.

After a day skating on the precipices of the market, ex-sergeant Phelan expressed confidence in Wall Street's ability to take care of itself. The system "has shown its ability to handle an increasing amount of volatility," he commented. Phelan's reassurance made for good public relations. But the market's volatility on Tuesday came within a hair of halting all trading.

A confidence crisis developed among retired folks. People who were living on pensions or income from lifetime savings were afraid that the stocks in their funds had been mortally wounded. They telephoned their pension or investment offices seeking reassurances that their payments would not be reduced. This time, most money managers were unable to calm their fears. Speaking of the crash, Fred Zuckerman, vice president and treasurer of Chrysler Corporation, said: "Clearly it's had a negative impact on the value of pension funds. But it certainly does not have any impact on meeting pension obligations."

Only a few pensioners believed him. Most knew that the border between pension-fund values and payments from those funds is thin indeed.

The Presidential Task Force on Market Mechanisms summarized the events in language stronger than is usually found in government reports. The report said, "Although Monday was the day of the dramatic stock market decline, it was midday Tuesday that the securities markets and the financial system approached breakdown. First, the ability of securities markets to price equities was in question. The futures and stock markets were disconnected. There were few buyers in either market and individual stocks ceased to trade. Investors began to question the value of equity assets."

Before Tuesday ended, stock market jokes were popping up on Broadway. "An armored car was robbed of $4 million in securities,"

Mort Sahl told his audience in the Neil Simon Theater. "The street value was $29,000."

How About Dinner Tonight?

In a future time on Wall Street, a rumor was generating.

"You know that cute little chick who works in the vice president's office? I bumped into her in the hall a couple of minutes ago, and boy did she look tired. She said she'd been typing till midnight, and they got a big meeting scheduled for five o'clock this evening."

"Yeah. So what? You invited?"

"Hell, no. But she told me about the memos they were typing. It's hot stuff. They're going to cut the dividends. The way the market dropped, our stock yields now are almost 70 percent higher than they were before the crash."

"Wait a minute. How come they're higher? You know I'm just a clerk trainee around here, and there's a lot of things I don't understand."

"Simple. The company pays $1.25 in dividends per share. When the stock price was $31.25 before the crash, that worked out to a dividend yield of four percent. Now the price plopped down to $18.75 and that puts the dividend yield up to 6.7 percent. Figure it out. Divide the dividend by the price, and you get the yield."

"Well, I haven't got a calculator with me, but I'll take your word for it. You've been around a while."

"They claim that 6.7 percent yield is too high. So they're going to cut the dividend payment to 75 cents. That'll keep the yield right on four percent, just where it was before the crash. Boy, but that's going to be tough on the old widowers and the pensioners. They're the ones who need the cash."

"Wow. That sounds bad."

"Well, that's what the little chick typed up, and that's why they're going to meet."

The rumors are about to start.

"I got to run. I got some phone calls to make before it's too late."

"Me, too."

"Say, wonder if that chick would like dinner tonight? Think I'll try to hit her up."

"Hey, wait a minute. I'm the guy who's been talking her up."

PROGRAM TRADING: THE GREAT DEBATE

Did program trading cause the October crash? Well, programs certainly became one of the whipping boys. The introduction of computers into securities markets a few years earlier enabled traders to execute massive complex transactions in seconds. Managers could program computer systems to buy or sell large blocks of stocks automatically when their prices reached or fell to a specific, preset level. Using program techniques, managers of large stock portfolios owned by insurance companies, mutual funds and pension funds established highly sophisticated trading techniques to protect the value of their shares. That's portfolio insurance, protecting stock investments against losses.

Another breed of investors, the arbitrageurs, attempts to make split-second profits. Seated in a room before a bank of screens that display stock prices from markets across the nation and around the world, arbitrageurs play one market against another. They sell in one market and buy in another. Their aim is to earn profits by trading on momentary price differences in two markets. If they know their math, arbitrageurs can play the game with little risk and earn high profits.

A single transaction in portfolio insurance or arbitrage means trading millions of shares in seconds—speeds and volumes that only computers can handle. The October crash was the first major market crisis to occur since vast computer networks were installed and wired to connect dealers to markets across the nation and around the world. Because of their size, and perhaps because their operational details and full impact on the market was not understood, program trading became an easy target to blame for the crisis.

But, contrary to wide public opinion and some government reports, the evidence that we have collected finds program trading largely innocent of charges placed against it. To blame the crash on program trading is akin to executing the messenger who delivers bad news. Certainly during the crisis, Wall Street computers did carry out large stock-selling orders in deluge after deluge, driving prices down with sledgehammer blows. But the computers were not necessarily performing program trading in its classic style. Several facts suggest that the crisis crippled markets to such an extent that normal program trading could not and did not work.

In our research, we have found considerable evidence that program trading often failed to perform as originally designed and was largely discarded on October 19 and 20, the crash's two biggest days. Many large portfolio managers had become fully invested in arbitrage positions during the market's high volatility in the previous week. These managers had exhausted their liquidity, their available cash or credit. Furthermore, the split-second market information that arbitrageurs require to carry out program trading simply did not exist during the crash. Stocks were being sold so rapidly and in such vast quantities as to cause delays up to one hour and more in reporting those transactions on tickers and screens. Computer screens act like a newspaper's front page that is being updated constantly with the new statistics that traders need before they can act. But the flow of information became fragmented and useless during the crash, and at several points computer screens blacked out.

Compounding the problem, a number of blue-chip shares were not being traded at all, because they attracted too few buyers or sellers to clear the market. The key indexes used by traders, the Dow Jones Industrial Average and the Standard & Poor's 500, were incorrect during many hours on October 19 and 20 because the information on which they are computed was out-of-date, incomplete or nonexistent. Recognizing this breakdown in the delivery of information, key market players often gave up on the indexes. Arbitrage program trading requires high-quality and timely information. As one arbitrageur told us: "No information, no arbitraging."

The government's General Accounting Office looked closely into the problems experienced by arbitrageurs during the crash. "Simultaneous buying and selling [i.e., arbitrage] under panic conditions was virtually impossible," the Accounting Office concluded. "Some leading stocks were not trading, and some stock prices as well as stock-index values were inaccurate. These conditions made index arbitrage impossible, because it was difficult to determine the true relationship between the cash market prices and futures prices."

On October 20 the New York Stock Exchange told its members not to use the highly computerized Designated Order Turnaround (DOT) system for program trading. DOT computers constitute one of the primary tools for the quick execution of large stock transactions, the key to successful arbitraging. One self-regulatory official said that arbitrage could be performed only by firms that could deliver stock orders manually to stock exchange trading posts. But some brokers were unable to shift from computers to a manual system. In any event, manual trading is painfully slow.

Success in program trading requires almost unlimited amounts of cash or credit. But the liquidity of many traders had evaporated during the previous week, and no new funding sources volunteered to stick out their necks. Program-trading strategies "presuppose perfect liquidity in the marketplace which was nonexistent on October 19 and 20," said the General Accounting Office, the Congressional watchdog agency.

Instead of causing the crash, arbitrage might have brought the market under control if it had been able to function properly, some traders believe. This view was reported by investigators from the General Accounting Office who said some investors told them that "had firms been able to engage in arbitrage activity, this might have helped keep prices in the futures and stock markets more in balance with each other, providing a measure of stability to the markets."

Portfolio insurance, the other practice in program trading, found itself in just as much trouble as arbitrage. Portfolio insurance is misnamed. It is not as reliable as life insurance. Unfortunately, portfolio insurance can collapse precisely at the moment when the stocks it insures are dying. That's what happened in October. In a falling market, portfolio insurance involves selling stock-index futures, rather than the securities themselves. Indexes can be traded faster and with less commission costs than the stocks they represent. Thus, indexes make an ideal property in which to deal. In theory, profits earned in trading indexes compensate for losses in the stock. But to sell an index, the trader must find a buyer. And on Monday and during the crisis hours on Tuesday, the market was filled with sellers, while buyers were scarce. That fact alone shut down much of the portfolio insurance.

Portfolio insurance also requires that indexes of future stock prices be synchronized closely with the actual trading price of the underlying stocks. If wide gaps develop between future and current cash prices, insurance systems falter. That's what happened on October 19 and 20. Because selling accelerated to superhigh speeds, futures and cash prices were not tracking each other properly. One user of portfolio insurance told the General Accounting Office that "his firm stopped trading on October 19 because futures appeared mispriced relative to stocks, but it was not clear which pricing was correct."

While program trading, including arbitrage and portfolio insurance, usually works under normal market conditions, it does not work in volatile markets when information is lacking and liquidity does not exist. Also, program trading does not work when everybody attempts to use it at the same time. In a catastrophic situation, a trader needs insurance badly. But that is precisely when portfolio insurance fails, just as health insurance sometimes fails when a catastrophic illness strikes.

Many market professionals believe that portfolio insurance, while responsible for not starting the crash, may have accelerated the stock market decline once it started. This analysis develops two points:

- In the previous week, institutional investors realized that the market was too volatile to deal in stock indexes as a method of insuring their stocks. So they started selling the stocks. On Monday, in search of other damage-control measures, they switched from stocks into bonds or into good old cash.
- The other point was psychological. Traders became fearful that the use of portfolio-insurance strategies by institutional investors would accelerate the market decline. To save their necks, traders rushed to sell their stocks.

The General Accounting Office learned that some market participants "blamed the institutions for panicking, adopting a 'sell at any cost mentality,' and trying to unwind in one day positions that may have taken up to a year to build."

Figures compiled by the Presidential Task Force disclose that mutual funds were the largest sellers of stocks on the New York Exchange on October 19 and 20. The mutuals sold $3.9 billion worth of shares. Sales made by portfolio insurers totaled $2.4 billion. Arbitrageurs sold $1.9 billion. Both insurance and arbitrage sales declined substantially on Tuesday from Monday's level, another indication that program trading was on the wane through the crisis that started in the previous week.

In an analysis published in the May/June 1988 issue of the *Harvard Business Review*, one of the authors of this book and two colleagues described how program trading actually improved market efficiency during the 1987 crash. They wrote:

"Many of those investigating the crash, among them the Presidential Task Force on Market Mechanisms, have suggested that program trading accelerated, or even triggered, a significant downfall following the initial price decline.

"It is hard to separate the price impact of programmed transactions from regular transactions even with a detailed, minute-by-minute record of price and volume information...In view of the magnitude of the crash and the amount of money involved, it is unlikely that major institutional investors simply allowed their computers to run rampant. Most likely, executives were constantly informed about stock price and volume and changed their strategy to meet the crisis as best they could.

"Nevertheless, our analysis cannot reject the possibility that program trading was responsible for part of the price decline and for a temporary overreaction. Our findings, however, indicate that if such a reaction took place, it did not move prices beyond what was justified by the fundamental conditions of the companies in question. At most, program trading may have accelerated a process of price adjustments that would and should have been triggered anyway. Stock prices were overvalued because of speculative buying before the crash. Program trading supplied the resounding slap to wake up the market by boldly pushing the system to its limit, but it was not the culprit. As in most other cases, it is wrong to blame the messenger.

"Our study suggests that program trading not only did not interfere with market rationality, but actually contributed to market efficiency by speeding up and completing the price adjustment process.

"The evidence...indicates that program trading played a critical role in compressing the crash to three days, during which prices declined 26.2 percent as measured by the Dow.

"The Dow, whose components are most widely used in program trading, collapsed in three days, while the equally weighted Wilshire index, which is dominated by stocks not traded under programs, took ten days to hit bottom...

"Program trading creates ideal conditions for an instantaneous flow of funds across markets and across financial instruments, with almost no budget constraints or any other barriers. All these characteristics are consistent with market efficiency.

"New technology in computers and communications has created a worldwide market with immense volume and a plethora of financial instruments. Program trading restrictions in such case may postpone price adjustments within and across capital markets, but

they cannot prevent those changes from occuring. The biggest effect
of restrictions, therefore, would be to impede market efficiency. If
this is true, why limit program trading at all?"

Chinese Firewater
*Our three traders for a major mutual fund, the fellows who weren't
thrilled by Luigi's wine list on that Friday night in the future, are now
trying the fiery white mao-tai in a Chinese restaurant.*

"Damn, but this stuff really kicks."

"Yeah, it does."

"Man, did we show those bastards, or did we show those bastards? We left a couple of those funds screaming for mercy. Took us
about two days, but we sure cleaned out the losers and got 'em into
Treasuries."

"Wonder what those professors who invented program trading
are doing tonight?"

"Probably in the library, reading Socrates or Einstein."

"Hell, no. I bet you if I were a professor I'd be asking some fresh-
man broad if she needs any help with her homework."

"Yeah, sure, you would. And you'd probably catch a fast one from
some gal who was majoring in judo with a specialty in kicking. Jesus.
This Chinese stuff really burns. Maybe we ought to go back to Luigi's."

"Well, we shouldn't be too tough on the profs. They got us a good
idea, portfolio insurance, working up the S&P to save our ass on the
stocks. Trouble is nobody trusts anyone around here when the shit's flying."

"Yeah, guess we tossed some of it in the fan ourselves."

"The system fell apart. What we need is a little milk of human
kindness, and a hell of a lot more trust to keep things working the
way they should."

"Milk? What, mixed with this firewater? At least that upstate
New York rotgut didn't make my eyes water."

DISMANTLING THE PROGRAMS

Program trading itself was not responsible for the crash. Quite the
opposite. In a paradoxical way, the price correction was accelerated
because program trading was dismantled, and their stocks dumped.
In a normal market, arbitrage and portfolio insurance work
smoothly. But during the week before Black Monday, stock prices

had fallen sharply, wiping out more than $300 billion in stock values. This convinced a few major market players, the managers of large institutional portfolios, that program trading, particularly portfolio insurance, was not working. So, during the weekend before Black Monday, they decided to save their investments by selling at any price. And that is what some big institutional investors did on Monday and Tuesday.

Evidence that eliminates program trading as a primary factor in the crash comes from the American Stock Exchange, the over-the-counter market, and practically every major stock exchange in the world. Outside the New York Stock Exchange, program trading is little used if at all. Yet the market crash was not limited to the New York Stock Exchange. Even where program trading was not practiced, stocks plummeted. Without the benefit of computer programs, prices collapsed on the American Exchange, the over-the-counter market, and stock exchanges all around the world.

Remember, people control computers. When stock prices move significantly away from their intrinsic values, human judgment takes over to buy or sell the mispriced stocks. If program trading developed some temporary mispricings, that situation was corrected by traders who were shopping for value. We saw that demonstrated when corporations bought back their own stock. We can not blame the computers.

Program trading is not evil, and we do not believe that it caused the crash. But, without a doubt, program trading did accelerate the speed of the crash once it started, and compressed the time in which it occurred. Although the 1987 market collapse was the most severe ever, it also was the shortest.

THE CHOSEN FEW

The Presidential Task Force uncovered an interesting point that illustrates the power and influence wielded by a relatively few big institutional investors on Wall Street. "One of the factors that was prevalent from Thursday through Tuesday was the concentration of buying and selling activity by a small number of large investors," the presidential investigators reported.

This concentration reached its peak on Black Monday. On that day of record volume, a mere ten sellers accounted for 15 percent of all sales on the New York Exchange. And ten buyers transacted nine percent of the purchases. The chosen few were even more active in the futures market: Ten buyers and sellers handled between 25 and 26 percent of Monday's total volume.

During the critical days of the crash, the big-money guys were selling to *escape from program trading* and searching for another way to cut their losses.

THE ANATOMY OF A CRASH

Typically, epic events in world economies—and we must remember that the October crash took place on five continents—are not caused by a single factor.

The Great Depression grew from many roots: World War I, the Allied war debts, German war reparations, erection of international trade barriers, excessive stock market speculation, decline in consumer buying, inadequate controls and regulation of the banking and securities industries, fundamental weaknesses in farming, faulty government monetary and fiscal policies in the early stages of the depression and the wonderful feeling that the gay and prosperous years of the 1920s would last forever. Let us toast the flapper girls with bathtub gin!

And so it was in October 1987. Wall Street was battered by many forces: unsound speculation, a wave of wild creative finance, climbing interest rates, high deficits in both the national budget and international trade, threats of inflation, America's low productivity, uncertainties over where currency-exchange rates were going, low personal savings in the United States compared with other industrial nations, threats that new tax regulations would cancel important tax benefits in corporate takeovers, war clouds over the Persian Gulf, the inability of various capital markets to act in synchronization and a growing concern that the administration in Washington lacked the courage or wisdom to lead America through dangerous shoals.

These problems were not new. They had been around for a long time before October. But in October, several sharply focused events occurred within a few days of each other. The close timing of these events may have been sufficient to set in motion what Wall Street long had expected and euphemistically spoke of as a market correction. In filtering out possible causes of the October crash, we believe that the most immediate triggers would include:

- Increasing interest rates.
- Realization by investors that the market was overvalued.
- Washington's announcement that the trade deficit was not declining as fast as had been expected.
- An impression from Treasury Secretary Baker's public statements that international monetary exchange agreements were not working.
- Escalating warfare in the Persian Gulf.
- Threatened withdrawal of tax benefits in corporate takeovers.

Just as a magnifying glass focuses the sun's rays on paper, several events converged in October with sufficient intensity to start a fire. In the words of the U.S. General Accounting Office, the crash "was caused by a confluence of macroeconomic, political, psychological and trading factors, and that isolating any one cause would be difficult."

The crash was caused by a number of fundamental factors. But rational financial theories employed by investors did not collapse. What really failed was the market mechanism, the system that is supposed to maintain an orderly market under any conditions.

WALL STREET AND THE HASIDIC JEWS

On New York City's West 47th Street, Jewish men of the orthodox Hasidic sect, which traces its origin back to Jewish mystics in eighteenth-century Poland, ply their trade. Whether it's summer or winter, they wear black hats, long black coats and white shirts without neckties, a uniform as distinctive as military dress. They conduct America's major diamond market. They buy and sell millions of dollars' worth of diamonds every day with, it is said, complete trust in their brothers' word. No sales contracts are signed. No attorneys witness their transactions. They strike a bargain orally and consummate the deal with a handshake, completely confident that their brothers' word is as solid and pure as the diamonds they sell. Seldom is the trust broken, perhaps because the Hasidics live and work in a tight-knit community where family ties are strong.

Hasidics are pragmatic. They know that the best way, if not the only way, to run their business is through trust. The same is true for Wall Street. Without mutual trust, no capital market can survive. But when markets crash, mutual trust suffers. Bankers refuse to extend lines of credits to their oldest customers. Fund managers fear that their portfolios will be shot down by reckless selling by their colleagues. Unlike a diamond, a stock certificate has no intrinsic value beyond faith and confidence in the issuing corporation. That confidence is based on perceptions, expectations and perhaps even pies in the sky—nothing tangible. But a diamond never loses its value.

When caught in illegal acts, inside traders and their suppliers of private information have been known to turn into informers to save their skins and their safe-deposit boxes. The stakes are high on Wall Street. A fortune can come or vanish in seconds. Greed interferes with prudence and good judgment. For years, under normal conditions, the trust system worked reasonably well on Wall Street. But, under crisis conditions, trust collapsed. Wall Street is not the ideal environment in which to maintain confidence in your competitors or even in your colleagues. They might want to stand on their promises. But when their portfolios face losses in the millions of dollars, they will act for their own best interests.

With a code of ethics centuries old and strong communal ties, Hasidic diamond dealers probably would retain mutual trust even under catastrophic conditions. At least their diamonds are not shedding value. Stock market players do not belong to a communal sect. They are just good old American capitalists, and rugged individualists. Their methods of operations are based on trust. Million-dollar deals are transacted over the telephone without even a handshake. But in a crisis, an atmosphere of fear replaces trust. Traders start questioning the solvency and honesty of their colleagues. It's everyone for themselves.

It's no wonder. Wall Street is operating with highly leveraged positions using other people's money. The 1987 crash developed a severe liquidity crisis, chaotic information, trading systems that did not work, rumors and fear. Mutual trust wilted.

8

Wednesday, October 21

FROM THE UNITED NATIONS TO UNITED ECONOMIES

In his own way, Pu Shan, director of the Institute of World Politics and Economy in Beijing, China, casts himself as a stock market analyst. His Communist nation provides modest opportunities to judge how economies are performing. For example, China's one securities market, the Shanghai Stock Exchange, lists only six shares. Trading is slower than a chess match. But when a reporter asked him, Pu was prepared to discuss the world situation in stocks.

Pu viewed Wall Street as a gambling center. The crash in the United States, he said, was the inevitable consequence of a "casino economy." He went on to say that the plunge of prices on the New York and other world exchanges had been expected for some time. Pu made his comments in an interview published in the *China Daily* newspaper in Beijing, where, nearly a century earlier, the last empress in the Manchu Dynasty ordered that all newspaper editors be arrested and punished "with the utmost rigor of the law."

The Shanghai Stock Exchange survived Black Monday unscathed. Its six shares traded quietly, if at all, while every other exchange in Asia, Australia, Europe and America were wrenched in turmoil.

In Japan they trade big. Encouraged by an apparent end to the Wall Street crisis, investors on the Tokyo Stock Exchange traded 1.1

billion shares on Wednesday, pushing the Nikkei Stock Average up by 9.3 percent after yesterday's record plunge of 14.9 percent.

Japan's highly skilled bureaucrats, the real power brokers in its conservative government, breathed more easily. The earlier decline could have resulted in a loss of up to $3.6 billion in one of the nation's most ambitious plans to sell a government monopoly to private stockholders. Two million shares of Nippon Telegraph and Telephone Corporation, the world's most highly capitalized and most expensive stock, were scheduled to go on sale within a few days. The government would use the receipts to finance construction of public-works projects designed to improve the quality of life in Japan, where, despite its national prosperity, many homes still lack flush toilets. The United States had been urging Japan to stimulate its domestic economy by building more roads, houses, sewage systems and other creature comforts while decreasing its economic dependence on exports. The Reagan administration believed that the U.S. trade deficit would shrink if the Japanese reversed the direction of their economic growth, turning it inward.

The highly priced stock in the government-owned telephone system plunged $1,800 a share earlier in the week, a drop of about $3.6 billion in the selling price of the stock offer. But the stock regained most of its value today, closing at the astronomical price of 2.8 million yen per share, about $19,404.

With world markets settling down at midweek, leaders in Kabuto-cho, Tokyo's financial district, were claiming a considerable share of the credit and expressing supreme confidence in Japan's place in the sun.

"There's a consensus that Tokyo has a leadership role among the world's stock markets and that we can contribute to calming them by being level-headed," said Takeshi Imamura, manager of the equities department at Daiwa Securities Company.

Nobumitsu Kagami, chief economist for the Nomura Investment Management Company, saw Japan exercising singular influence over other nations: "People are still inclined to think that whatever happens in the rest of the world, the Japanese market will resist it."

America's decline into a debtor nation was very much in mind. "Japan is the world's leading creditor nation," said Hironobu Hagio, chief portfolio manager for Nissei BOT Capital Management Corporation. "We have the money. We should just relax and buy stocks. That will have a very positive influence on world markets."

Brave, bullish talk dominated Tokyo. "Of course I have my Japanese bias, but our interest rates are the lowest in the world, and our financial institutions are loaded with cash," said Keiji Yasuda, manager of the international department at New Japan Securities Company. "Japan should take responsibility in stopping this global vicious circle of panic."

But on Wall Street, U.S. and Japanese security firms reported that Japanese investors were slower than Europeans in investing their money in American stocks after Black Monday. "They are stepping back and taking a look," reported a spokesperson for the New York subsidiary of Nomura Securities, the world's largest brokerage house. But Japan remained a significant force on Wall Street. In just two years, Japanese investments in foreign stocks had soared by 70 times. In 1986, Japanese invested about $7 billion in foreign stocks, 90 percent of it in the United States. In 1984, stock purchased overseas by Japanese added up to only $100 million. In 1985 it totaled $1 billion.

In Europe, postcrash market behavior reflected a mirror image of Wall Street: confusion and nervousness, followed by euphoria as prices recovered so rapidly that electronic systems could not cope. European markets rocketed upward at velocities that almost broke the information systems. In London, the *Financial Times* index of 100 leading stocks gained 142.2 points, a rise of eight percent, breaking the previous point record of 48.6 set on May 8. Heavy trading strained the index so severely that its figures were unavailable for three hours during the middle of the day. In Frankfurt, prices climbed during some of the heaviest trading in memory, and the stock exchange had to remain open an extra hour to process orders. The Brussels Bourse could not complete calculating its closing price index until the next morning. Trading continued in Paris, Milan and Zurich beyond the normal hours.

All across Western Europe, stocks returned to life. Reacting vigorously, traders were inspired to buy, not only by Tuesday's Wall Street recovery, but also by signs that interest rates would be lowered and by the tempting bargain prices on shares created by their early week declines. Gains in one market touched off bullish reactions in another country.

The old domino theory, describing how one nation's fate falls onto its neighbor, never did work out politically as Washington had warned. Despite dire predictions from several U.S. administrations in the 1950s and 1960s, falling dominoes did not spread communism through all of Southeast Asia. Communism won the nations of Indochina but, except in isolated pockets, never reached Thailand, Burma, Malaysia or Singapore. Castro's communism never spread in the Caribbean nor to Florida.

In economics, however, the domino theory functions. Cheap production costs in one country bankrupt competitors in another country. Advanced technology in East Asia destroys the value of goods produced in Europe. Interest rates increase in America, and Japan buys U.S. bonds. The stock that crashes on Wall Street is a shot heard 'round the world. Nothing proved the economic domino theory better than the stock market crash of October 1987 that spread from nation to nation.

National economies today are interlocked far more than political systems ever were. Consider the attempts to organize nations into world bodies for peace. The League of Nations collapsed in the 1930s while wars were fought in China, Spain and Ethiopia. Although President Wilson was one of its architects, Republican opponents in the U.S. Senate voted against league membership in 1919 and 1920. Today, the United Nations stumbles in its search for a common approach to world problems. But each year, united economies are gluing nations closer and closer together. Never again can nations live in isolation as the United States did between the two world wars. Whether we like it or not, there's a Toyota in America's future.

In its study of the October crash, the U.S. General Accounting Office reported to the Congress in January 1988: "While international financial flows are not recent developments, their importance is growing and the links among the financial systems of different nations are becoming stronger."

Black Monday, its antecedents and its consequences, dramatically illustrated the depths to which economies have become internationalized. The domino theory works. When one stock market falls, it knocks over its neighbors.

NEEDED: A NEW HARMONY

Since the late 1970s, traders in currencies, commodities and common stock have been staffing 24-hour trading desks. On world markets the day never ends. Trading continues someplace in the world at every hour. One international news agency, United Press International, defined its mission as: "Deadline Every Minute." It's the same with the markets. Financial forces know no national borders, and they take no holidays. As we saw so clearly in October 1987, the markets of the world constantly interact with each other.

On the other side of the globe, while America sleeps, the Tokyo Stock Exchange helps create the coming day on Wall Street and in the City in London. To deal with the internationalization of markets, the night watch has been set in New York, London, Tokyo, Sydney and most major trading places. Someone is always on duty at a financial post, because the economic destiny of all of us is related to every corner of the earth. No longer is any nation an island, entire of itself.

Yet nobody controls, coordinates or regulates the highly complicated and vulnerable network of international financial trading. It seems unlikely, probably impossible, that nations will ever agree to join in a world authority on international financial transactions. Decisions relating to interest and exchange rates affect the livelihood of every man, woman and child. Few political leaders would pass the authority to influence economies at home into the hands of a world body.

But perhaps nations can increase their efforts to bring interest and exchange rates into better international harmony and agree on some controls and coordination of trading procedures. Interest hikes in West Germany and Japan contributed to destabilizing Wall Street. In October 1987 we saw for the first time the intimate relationship that had developed between stock exchanges in various countries. Now we must observe, investigate and identify all strengths and weaknesses in international transactions, and learn more about how one component influences the other and how to avoid a downward spiral around the world. Capital markets now are largely borderless. If new regulations are imposed in one country, capital simply will move to a less restrictive nation.

P. T. Barnum, the nineteenth-century circus genius, developed the greatest show on earth by putting a multitude of magnificent acts under one tent. In addition to his traveling circus, he collected strange, exotic and wonderful exhibits for display in Barnum's American Museum in New York City before the Civil War.

In his 1855 autobiography, *The Life of P. T. Barnum Written by Himself*, Barnum reported that the "attractions of the Museum have been greatly diversified. Industrious fleas, educated dogs, jugglers, automatons, ventriloquists, living statuary, tableaux, gypsies, albinos, fat boys, giants, dwarfs, rope-dancers, caricatures of phrenology, and 'live Yankees,' pantomime, instrumental music, singing and dancing in great variety, including Ethiopians."

All that in one building for 25 cents. More than a century later the American financial system found itself in great trouble because it was broken into separate acts without a ringmaster to synchronize the show. Futures are traded in Chicago to protect stocks on Wall Street. But the two markets operate under different regulatory agencies. Trading on the Boston, Philadelphia and Pacific Exchanges develop economic forces that move levers in other markets. Powerful pressures are piped out of markets in London, Tokyo, Paris, Toronto and Hong Kong, driving prices up or down in other exchanges.

In its investigation of the October crash, the Presidential Task Force made this observation: "In many respects, the problems associated with the October market break can be traced to intermarket failure. Institutional and regulatory structures designed for separate marketplaces were incapable of dealing with a precipitate intermarket decline which brought the financial system to the brink."

Obviously, the various U.S. markets, based in different cities, are not performing under one roof as did Barnum's industrious fleas and dancing Ethiopians. But, in an ideal scene, America's futures and stock markets should be synchronized and act in harmony as if they were directed by one ringmaster. They failed to do so in October. Because systems for communicating information were running at least an hour and often several hours behind the unprecedented trading volume, one exchange did not know what another exchange was doing.

In the stock and futures markets, basic operating rules vary. Take margins, for example. The deposit required in one market to purchase stocks with borrowed funds is much higher than the margin that must be deposited in another market to trade in options or futures. "Should two margin requirements apply to what is, in effect, one market?" the Presidential Task Force asked. At another point, the White House commission said, "Although exchanges may not be pleased with the prospect of intermarket regulation, the Task Force has concluded it is essential to ensure the integrity of financial markets."

The Tea Arrives on Time
On the international scene, adopting uniform procedures for markets that, with each passing day, are becoming more closely interrelated

certainly would daunt the most skilled diplomat. But listen to a summit conference in the future between the president of the United States and the prime minister of Japan:

"Mr. Prime Minister, our two nations have made much progress in removing some of the last impediments in opening our markets to each other. My constituents are particularly pleased with your decision to import orange juice."

"Ah, so, Mr. President."

"Mr. Prime Minister, my Treasury Department is grateful to you and your government for your firm stand on interest rates in your country."

"Ah, so, Mr. President."

"We seem to have leveled off with currency exchange rates that are acceptable to both of our business communities."

"Ah, so."

"But my friends in the stock market are concerned that the—how shall I say it?—the more-open rules on your stock exchange create the possibility of a high level of volatility in your market that would immediately upset our market, if you understand what I mean. Your market is the largest in the world. A sneeze in your market shakes my market like one of your earthquakes."

"Ah, so, Mr. President. You speak with good humor. Very good humor. [Pause] *The stock market? Hmmm. We must think about this. We've done so much already. The orange juice. It's become very popular in my country. Excellent taste. Send us more. [Pause] The stock market. Hmmm. We must discuss with many people."*

"You are correct, Mr. Prime Minister. My cabinet believes that we need uniform procedures and some coordinated regulations for all major markets of the world, not only yours and mine. They all are so closely interlinked. If we adopt regulations unilaterally in my country, investors might move their trade to another country. The negative results will bounce back to us, or perhaps to you, Mr. Prime Minister. All of our nations would lose control, and an international financial jungle would be created. We would lose business to the pirate markets of the world. The alternative of each nation restricting international investments in its own markets would result in even worse consequences. So perhaps we can place the issue of uniform procedures for all major markets on the next agenda for the Group of 11. We heads of the major industrial nations do seem to be making some progress when we meet each year."

"Ah, so. But it was easier to work when we were only G-7 instead of G-11."

"No doubt that you are correct, Mr. Prime Minister. Or even better, back when we were a cozy G-5. How times have changed. [A sigh.] When was it? In 1988, I believe, when China bought its first steel plant in my country. Now look at them today."

"Ah, so, Mr. President. I know. They're becoming highly competitive in microchips. But about this stock market business. Where can we find a precedent for international controls that might lead to a degree of uniformity among market mechanisms in our various countries? It does seem difficult."

"No problem, Mr. Prime Minister. We set the pattern at the Congress of Berne in 1874."

"Excuse me, Mr. President. 1874? My country at that time was—how shall I say it?—becoming acquainted with the world outside our shores."

"At Berne in 1874, we signatory nations agreed to form a single territory for the purposes of postal communication under the Universal Postal Union. Now almost every nation accepts its principles."

"Ah, so. Very interesting, Mr. President. A Universal Stock Union? Interesting. A single territory for all our stock markets? Ah, so. Ah, so. [A long pause.] Mr. President. The tea has arrived."

THE NEW INTERNATIONAL DIMENSION

In its January 1988 report to Congress, the General Accounting Office made the very recommendation discussed above by our fictional president and prime minister.

The report said: "October demonstrated that domestic market emergencies are linked to trading around the world. They cannot be addressed solely by domestic authorities. Moreover, solutions posed for domestic problems could affect the international competitive position of U.S. financial markets. The Fed should clearly be involved in formulation of solutions to the problems of international emergencies because of its international expertise and relationships."

Summing up the international issue in one sentence, the SEC said in its postcrash report: "The events of October 1987 brought to the forefront the degree to which events in one market can affect other markets and emphasize the need for greater international co-operation and initiatives."

A PROPOSAL IN TOKYO

In August 1988 the chairman of the New York Stock Exchange, John J. Phelan, Jr., visited the only stock market in the world that is bigger than his own, the Tokyo Stock Exchange. He used his visit to recommend a first step toward some degree of international cooperation in policing the securities industry.

Speaking to members of the Foreign Correspondents Club of Japan, Phelan suggested that common worldwide definitions of insider trading be established in an effort to combat unscrupulous traders and to reassure investors. He made his remarks while several cases of insider-trading deals were being investigated in Japan, where the rules are less restrictive than in the United States. Some forms of insider trading are acceptable in Japan.

"Everybody comes from different cultures and corporate backgrounds," Phelan said. "But the users of those markets have to see that those markets are fair and that they are not disadvantaged to work in them."

He proposed that each market establish its own definition of insider trading and then work together to set up common rules. "Insider trading is a virus, and it spreads. In time it will cast a shadow over this [Tokyo] market, and that will create a drive toward fairness."

Phelan announced in Tokyo that Japanese officials had formed the Japan Advisory Committee to counsel the board of the New York Stock Exchange on Japanese business and on the relationships between international capital markets.

The Mathematical Disaster
Before our hypothetical big crash of the future, one nation worked out a set of mathematical formulas to defend its economic borders and crush competitors abroad. It came about this way. After inventing portfolio insurance, a number of financial scholars turned their research toward developing equations to forecast the precise impact on foreign trade caused by altering interest and foreign exchange rates. In the 1980s central banks could only guess whether and by how much their international trade balance would improve if they devalued their currency.

Using a supercomputer to work out her equations, a scholar in nation A discovered that a 1.3 percent decrease in interest rates and a currency devaluation of 2.6 points would give personal computers manufactured in her nation enough of an international price edge to knock out country B's computer business. Other mathematical coefficients were involved in this complex game that measured the cost of procuring materials for personal computers in country C, manufacturing certain parts in country D and other parts in country E, shipping all parts to country F for assembling and then selling finished personal computers to the world at a price and quality level no other nation could match. Other percentage points for optimum interest and currency rates were computed for automobiles, electronics, aircraft, superconductors, biotechnology products, petroleum products and even fast foods.

While nation A was selling personal computers around the world, academic scholars in nation B devised a new type of virus: mathematical formulas that would enable banks in nation B to destabilize the interest and foreign exchange rates in nation A, the leader in personal computers.

Then nation Q a minor player on the world scene, called home one of its PhD candidates who had been studying in a university in nation A. He brought with him several mathematical secrets from nation A. After a year's work, he delivered to his prime minister an entirely new interest and currency formula that made it too costly for nation F, assemblers of personal computers for nation A, to import the food it desperately needed from nation Q And so forth.

Thus, instead of a tariff war, the world became involved in a mathematical modeling war that delivered heavy blows to the economies of nations A and Z, and all nations in between. This research, actually in progress by the 1980s, was applied recklessly by nations from A to Z, and made the trade wars of the 1930s look like a Ping-Pong match in comparison. Manipulations of currencies and interest rates left economies in shambles.

BIGGER THAN AL CAPONE

A few weeks before Black Monday, David S. Ruder, a mild-mannered law professor, left the campus of Northwestern University to become the chief regulator of the nation's financial markets.

During the confirmation hearing, several senators spoke against President Reagan's appointment of Ruder to the chairmanship of the Securities and Exchange Commission. They questioned whether Ruder would aggressively enforce regulations that control stock trading. Some senators believed that the regulatory processes of the SEC were weak and that the administration was interfering as little as possible in Wall Street operations.

"While Mr. Ruder may well have respected academic credentials, he is simply not the right person for the SEC," Senator Terry Stanford, a Democrat from North Carolina, said on the floor of the chamber on August 7, 1987. "Certainly, at a time when the SEC desperately needs a strong enforcer, the White House has instead put forward a man whose commitment to enforcement can only be called wanting." During confirmation hearings, Ruder supported an SEC position that opposed new legislative restrictions on corporate raiders and takeovers. For months, public attention had been focused on hostile acquisitions of corporations by outsiders, and illegal stock trading by persons possessing inside information on a company's performance and its future plans. In government and business, voices were being raised to support stricter controls on the securities industry. Critics charged that stock markets had indeed, as Pu Shan said in China, degenerated into a great gambling game in which players disregarded the welfare of a corporation and its employees, and ruthlessly piled up profits won in all sorts of imaginative stock deals.

In recent years television and newspapers have cut through the esoteric operations of the securities industry, little understood by anyone except the experts, and turned the stock market into a page-one crime story. Wall Street plots read bigger than the exploits of bootlegger Al Capone or bank robber John Dillinger. On Wall Street, the take was counted in the billions of dollars. Not street punks, but millionaire businesspeople, educated in respectable universities, were being handcuffed by police and led out of their luxurious offices to a lockup.

This new stock market saga become so pervasive in American society that Hollywood produced one of the first movies to probe the intricacies of Wall Street, salting it with sufficient sex to satisfy a popular image of yuppies. Appropriately named *Wall Street*, the film enjoyed a bullish career, in large measure because its release happily coincided with the October crash.

The dean of the law school at Northwestern University survived the Senate debate, and David Ruder's appointment to the SEC was confirmed by a vote of 81 to 17. He took office on August 7, 1987, replacing John S. R. Shad, who had become the United States ambassador to the Netherlands in June. Ruder, 58, a Phi Beta Kappa, was no stranger to Wall Street. From 1978 to 1982 he served on the legal advisory committee to the board of directors of the New York Stock Exchange. But perhaps nothing could have prepared him for Black Monday. He was in office just two-and-a-half months when the market crashed. The former professor almost failed his first test.

On the morning of Black Monday, reporters bombarded him with questions. With a candor more suited to the classroom than to a news conference, Ruder said that he had discussed the possibility of calling for a brief halt in Wall Street trading to calm the markets. Television and wire reports flashed his statement to financial markets, and some traders believed that operations would be suspended. Rather than calming the market, Ruder had fanned uncertainty. He tried to clarify his remarks, stating that he was speaking in general rather than specific terms.

Antennae on Wall Street are finely tuned to receive and amplify every piece of information that may affect market trends. The SEC watches Wall Street continuously, and vice versa. So sensitive is the SEC that it will not even disclose how many monitoring screens it employs in watching stock markets nor even disclose where they are located. The SEC knows that its every act, or anticipated act, can affect the market significantly.

After the crash, considerable criticism was leveled against Ruder and the SEC. Concern was expressed over Ruder's lack of working experience on Wall Street and whether he would demonstrate toughness in regulatory matters.

"His background isn't markets," said Democratic Representative Ron Wyden of Oregon. Other critics objected to Ruder's discussing the possibility of a temporary halt in trading on Black Monday, "an action that critics say would have caused more panic," *The Wall Street Journal* wrote. "The ill-timed comments left many people in Washington and on Wall Street with an impression of Mr. Ruder as a slightly dazed academic."

The October crash involved markets over which the SEC has no control: futures trading in the United States and stock markets overseas. Ruder commented, "This is the first time in market history that the first question every morning is: How did Tokyo do?" Separate from the SEC, the Commodity Futures Trading Commission regulates futures markets. But because futures and stocks now are traded in tandem, some experts believe that the two markets must be put under one regulatory agency to prevent an even worse crisis in the future.

Charges have been made that the SEC has not kept up with market growth in recent years. The SEC staff shrank from 1,982 members in 1981 to 1,898 in 1986. Some officials believe the productivity of the staff has been increased by using computers. Others disagree.

Craig Simmons directed the General Accounting Office's review of the SEC. After the crash, he said, "We think their [SEC's] resources have been outstripped by the market. Since 1980, the markets have exploded, the number of employees has skyrocketed and trading volume has gone off the scale. You've got to wonder if they [SEC] can handle it."

In any event, on Wednesday evening, after three days of market turmoil, Ruder issued an optimistic statement: "At this time, the industry is diligently responding to the extraordinary circumstances of the last three days. While there have been isolated firm failures and temporary operational difficulties, on balance the industry remains strong and the markets appear to be rebounding."

FOR ECONOMIC GROWTH, A NOBEL PRIZE

David Ruder's analysis hit the target. On this second day following Black Monday, markets rebounded in Asia and Europe, and Wall Street performed magnificently. President Reagan said the crisis appeared to be over. Trading shifted on Wednesday into a pattern that appeared to reflect a healthy, robust image of corporate America.

The recovery in stock prices on Tuesday had been limited to a few blue-chip securities of the type included in the Dow Jones and the Standard & Poor's indexes. But the vast majority of stocks continued to fall that day. On Tuesday, only 509 stocks gained in price while 1,445 declined. Strength in selected blue-chip issues may have been created by traders running for safety. Frightened by Monday, investors were looking for protective coverage under the wings of the largest and presumably the safest companies on the Big Board. They deserted the rest of corporate America.

But that was not the case on Wednesday. Price recoveries swept across the Big Board. A broad range of shares, representing many industries, gained on Wednesday, not just the bench-mark stocks that comprise the two principal indexes used to measure the market, the Dow Jones and the Standard & Poor's 500. On the New York Exchange, 1,749 shares advanced in price and only 209 lost. The Wilshire Index, which averages the prices of more than 5,000 stocks, rose 182.711 points to 2,553.125. That remarkable climb indicated that the total market value of stocks had increased by more than $182 billion on Wednesday.

In Wednesday's across-the-board action, the Dow Jones Average climbed 186.84 points to close at 2,027.85. That constituted a 10.1 percent advance, one of the largest percentage gains ever recorded on the New York Stock Exchange. In just two days, the Dow Jones had recaptured about half of its Black Monday losses.

Declining interest rates helped propel the stock rally. When interest rates climbed earlier in the year and surpassed stock earning-yields, bonds and other fixed-income investments became more attractive. But, with the help of the Federal Reserve's midcrash promise to provide liquidity, interest rates reversed and started declining. With interest rates down, stocks once again looked good.

By any standard, Wednesday's volume was heavy, 449.4 million shares, although less than on Monday or Tuesday, when trading topped 600 million shares each day. Each of those three days exceeded Wall Street's wildest dreams. In planning its future computer requirements, the exchange had forecast a daily volume by the end of 1987 of 400 million shares, 500 million shares in 1988, and 600 million shares by the end of 1990. Black Monday had catapulted the Big Board three years into the future.

To meet their future, copywriters for a number of banks and security houses worked through the night to prepare new advertisements that were in tune with the times.

By midweek, Chemical Bank had published an ad featuring the face of a bear to commemorate the fallen market. The caption read: "Chemical Bank. For People Who Are Finding the Market Unbearable." The ad suggested investments in Chemical's certificates of deposit.

On this Wednesday of monumental dealings on world stock market, the Nobel Committee saw fit to award its prize in economics to Robert M. Solow, 63, a professor at the Massachusetts Institute of Technology. In his research, Solow stressed that technology contributes as much to long-term economic growth as do capital and labor. In the stock market, the high technology of creative finance helped to generate the boom before the crash. But later, the high technology of program trading accelerated the disaster and compressed its time. A zero-sum game.

SHELL-SHOCKED IN WAR

In World War I, the condition was described as shell shock. Its victims were defended by their relatives who explained in whispered words, "You know, he was in the trenches."

They called it "battle fatigue" in the Second World War. On the morning of January 31, 1945, a few moments after 1000 hours, at Sainte-Marie-aux-Mines in France, where the snow was knee-deep, Private Eddie D. Slovik was executed by a 12-man firing squad. He was the only American soldier to be put to death for desertion since the Civil War.

In Korea, nearly every member of one small United States Army unit bugged out in battle, turned away from the enemy and fled. From Vietnam, gaunt, confused, silent men returned home to neighbors who believed that America had dishonored itself in Southeast Asia. Philip Caputo describes the syndrome of war neurosis eloquently in his novel *Indian Country.*

In the Great War, battle fatigue was popularly ascribed to continued concussion by artillery fire. Psychiatrists report that war neurosis manifests itself through many symptoms, including nightmares, sleeplessness, loss of appetite, dilated pupils, increased heart rate and excessive sweating.

The U.S. General Accounting Office said that the nation's entire financial system might have faced "massive disruptions" if the decline in stock prices had continued just one more day after Black Monday. In those first 19 days in October, the 30 Dow Jones stocks lost nearly $1 trillion and their self-confidence.

Shell-Shocked on Wall Street
In a year yet to come, on the second day of another crash, prices fall so sharply on rumors of inflation, deficits, farm failures, unemployment and interest hikes, combined with crashing markets abroad, that the value of stocks listed on the exchange plunges by around $1 bil-

lion in a single day. Or is it $2 billion? Nobody really knows. The information systems are so far behind trading that accurate calculations are impossible.

The chairman of the SEC is overwhelmed by market drops at home and abroad, and appalled at highly suspect activities on the futures market. "I have full control," he says. He repeats his claim of control many times, but says virtually nothing else, so that his words seem hollow.

The Federal Reserve System remains silent. Specialists are drained of all their financial resources after buying nearly $2 billion-worth of stocks that no one else wants. The wreckage on Wall Street is vast. But the nation's central bank, convinced that the market had been out of touch with reality before the crash and needed a significant correction, is unwilling to risk another dime in credit to the securities industry. To a frantic telephone call from one of his best Wall Street customers, the vice president of a major bank can only say, "I'm sorry." With no support from the Fed, banks are calling in earlier loans extended to Wall Street.

To cover his losses, one specialist offers to sell his seat on the exchange at a price he honestly describes as resembling a fire sale.

The market system is collapsing. Volatility has reached a level never before experienced. Prices on individual stocks are falling by ten and even 20 percent. Without cash or credit, fewer and fewer specialists are able to bend against the wind and to attempt to restore order by judicious buying and selling. Following the crowd, specialists try to sell off stocks from their own portfolios. The big securities houses, those upstairs firms with far more assets than floor specialists, either are selling from their own accounts or are sitting back hoping against hope that the market will stabilize. Many over-the-counter dealers have closed. Those still open can barely cope with the flood of telephone orders. Workers are exhausted and performing at about half their normal capacity.

The breakdown in the marketing process matches the 1987 crash but this time is much worse. (On the 1987 problem, the Presidential Task Force reported: "Market-makers possessed neither the resources nor the willingness to absorb the extraordinary volume of selling demand that materialized. . . The violence of the market movements, both upward and downward, threatened to undermine the integrity of the market and may have substantially inhibited buyers' participation.")

A U.S. Marine helicopter flies the president of the United States from the White House lawn to Bethesda Naval Hospital. The president's routine medical examination had been scheduled many days in advance. But rumors sweep the markets that the commander in chief had suffered a mild heart attack while being briefed by the secretary of the Treasury. While the president crosses the White House lawn to the helicopter, reporters shout questions, asking him what caused the crash. "I don't know anymore than you do," he replies. They ask what the government will do. The president replies, "I don't know."

With information screens blank, rumors fill the void:

"Hey, all the phones are dead at Stocks Unlimited, and some woman just told me their main door is locked."

"How does she know the door's locked?"

"Beats the hell out of me."

"Doesn't matter. Before the screens blacked out, the figures were so messed up I couldn't tell which way prices were going."

"Some nut in Treasury is blaming the Japanese for screwing up the market. He's got a statement on the wire over at the Post that the government is going to kick foreigners out of the market."

"Cripes! Nippon Unlimited was my best customer. Another Pearl Harbor."

"Buybacks? Nah, you're wrong on that one. Corporation buybacks stopped a couple of hours ago, at least. They've decided to wait for lower prices."

"Did you hear about Mutuals Unlimited? They've run out of cash on redemptions and can't sell enough to meet liquidation orders. They are trying to tell their call-in customers to wait for a big announcement being mailed out next week."

"What announcement?"

"Who knows? I bet Old Man Mutuals is trying to think it up right now."

A trader approaches a desk where one of his exhausted colleagues sits. They had been classmates in graduate business school, where they spent many long nights discussing future careers and the kind of women they would and would not marry.

"We're wiped out. We're out of business. Let's go down and have a beer at Joe's place."

Silence. No reply. The man sits at his desk and stares at the blank screen. How long had it been since that breakdown in the informa-

tion system had wiped his screen blank? One hour? Two hours? Or was it yesterday?

A pallor covers the man's face. His eyes stare as if unfocused and his face is as blank as his screen. His hands tremble. Cold neon lights from the ceiling reflect off the perspiration on his face.

"Come on. Let's get outside. Get some air."

Just before his head slumps forward in a faint, the man stutters and mumbles, but the sounds shape no words. In the hospital emergency room, the young doctor is cheery and reassuring. "A little shock. Maybe something he ate."

PATTERNS OUT OF CHAOS

Markets that trade in securities, futures, options and commodities have become interlocked into a vast network. Each trading point, in the United States and abroad, generates forces that drive prices up or down in other markets. Like waves in a turbulent sea, the economies of all nations pound against each other. Can the size and shapes of those wind-tossed waves be plotted in advance?

The science of chaos attempts to find patterns in what physicists call "nonlinear dynamical systems." They are dealing with such questions as whether the size and flow of bubbles in boiling water can be plotted in advance. In economics, researchers are trying to determine if the laws of mathematics will ever be able to forecast the directions that markets take.

Some economists believe they have discovered mathematical patterns in stock prices, market indexes, bond prices and other financial statistics. But others claim that markets resemble a random walk, and they question whether the new science of chaos—discovering predictable structures even in wild and erratic behavior—can be applied to Wall Street.

After the October crash, Kenneth J. Arrow, a Nobel laureate in economics at Stanford University, told *The New York Times:* "It is true that people who have been studying the stock market with the tools of nonlinear dynamics have found, before this last episode, evidence of chaotic behavior. It's tempting to jump from that to a statement about recent events, but I don't think anything can explain a fall of 20 percent in one day."

At New York University, economist James Ramsey says that stock market behavior cannot be analyzed by old methods. He says that financial experts on Wall Street are "observing behavior that begins to be amenable to the ideas of chaotic dynamics."

Immediately after the crash, Shelley Zacks, an applied mathematician at the State University of New York at Binghamton, tried to apply some mathematical chaos models to the market. They did not work. "A lot of research still has to be done, using huge data bases, before any conclusions about chaos theory and the market can be made seriously," Professor Zacks said.

If such a research breakthrough occurs, bankers, specialists, brokers and traders may someday find the stock market as predictable as a road map. But perhaps we always should expect a detour or two.

9

Thursday, October 22

"MR. PRESIDENT, WOULD YOU BUY STOCKS NOW?"

"Thank you, Mr. President."

Those words close presidential news conferences in the White House. Only one reporter is authorized to pronounce the closing benediction: the reporter who has served the longest on the presidential beat. For many years the senior reporter at the White House has been Helen Thomas. Born in Winchester, Kentucky, in 1920, Thomas joined the Washington staff of United Press International during World War II.

The White House normally allocates 30 minutes for President Reagan's news conferences. But if important questions remain, Helen Thomas has the privilege of extending the session a few minutes. Running overtime upsets the television networks, because it delays prime-time entertainment shows that are supported by million-dollar advertising budgets. White House news conferences are televised as a public service. But the opportunity to ask a few more questions delights print journalists.

When correspondents continue to shout questions after Thomas pronounces the ritualistic "Thank you, Mr. President," and the reporters often do, the president can leave those questions unanswered, saying that Helen Thomas has told him he is finished. That is what happened on Thursday night in the East Room of the White

House when Reagan held his first news conference since Black Monday. After Thomas delivered the benediction, reporters crowded around the president, asking at least eight questions. He demurred, saying, "Helen has told me that I'm through, that I have to leave here now." While Reagan backed out of the room, reporters, some shouting simultaneously, repeated one question: "Mr. President, would you buy stocks now?" He never answered.

But earlier, in reply to the first question in the news conference, Reagan had declared that the economy was sound. Employment figures were great, and double-digit inflation had been reduced, he said. He suggested that the stock market crash could lead to a recession only "if enough people without understanding the situation, panicked and decided to put off buying things that normally they would be buying, postponing purchases and so forth."

During the nationally televised news conference, Reagan did not attempt to diagnose the causes of the crash. But, after having "watched the stock market toss and turn," he suggested a "productive and constructive" procedure to deal with the national budget deficit. The unbalanced budget hardly qualified as a new problem. But in the eyes of many investors this week, the deficit played an important role in unraveling Wall Street. It could hardly be ignored. So the president announced that he would meet with congressional leaders to find ways to reduce the national budget deficit. Reagan said the deficit for the fiscal year that ended less than three weeks before Black Monday totaled $148 billion, a figure that was $73 billion lower than a year earlier.

The president told reporters and TV viewers across the country that Nicholas F. Brady, a New York investment banker, would head a Presidential Task Force to "examine the stock market procedures and make recommendations on any necessary changes."

But the President never did say whether he would buy stocks in October 1987.

Brady, 57, was cochairman of Dillon, Read and Company. In 1982 he completed an unexpired term in the U.S. Senate. Otherwise he had worked on Wall Street. He graduated from Yale and Harvard, and is a great-grandson of one of Thomas A. Edison's business associates.

Within a few months, the Brady Commission produced a detailed report on the October crash. "In hindsight, the Brady Report was the most definitive of all the studies after October," said Jeffrey B. Lane, president of Shearson Lehman Hutton.

Brady organized his experts and put them to work just a few days after the crash. Other postcrash studies were prepared by the Securities and Exchange Commission, the General Accounting Office and by the various exchanges. Each of these lengthy and detailed reports was studied carefully in the preparation of this book. In the summer of 1988, Brady was appointed secretary of the Treasury. He replaced James A. Baker III, who resigned to manage George Bush's presidential campaign.

After President Reagan's news conference, an opinion sampling conducted by *The New York Times* showed mixed reactions to Reagan's comments on the stock market crash.

Roger B. Smith, chairman and chief executive officer of General Motors, said: "The market has made it more clear than ever that the time for action on the budget deficit is now. With the President's statement tonight and those of congressional leaders, we think the stage has been set for realistic progress to be made."

Peter A. Cohen, chairman and chief executive of Shearson Lehman Hutton, said: "He should have had definitive ideas to deal (a) with the internal budget deficit and (b) with the external trade deficit. I was looking forward to hearing something very specific."

A NICE WEEK FOR THE HAVE-NOTS

When President Reagan, the Great Communicator, was talking about the stock markets, was he getting through to the 242,200,000 people in the United States? Did they really care about Wall Street? Was it important to them? What were they thinking on Main Street and Rural Route 1?

If a time capsule from October 1987 was opened in the year 2087, its newspapers, magazines and television scripts might suggest that Wall Street was a thoroughfare, extending from the East River across America's purple mountain majesties and fruited plains to the Golden Gate Bridge. The media always looks for a fresh story, anything new and exotic, to pump excitement into the 6 P.M. news or next morning's front page. In October 1987, press and broadcasters painted Wall Street so wide that it appeared to dominate all life in the United States.

At the time of the 1929 crash, 99 percent of Americans owned no stock. In 1988 about 80 percent of Americans were not direct stockholders and probably hadn't the faintest idea how to go about buying a share. But Black Monday and its aftermath was an editor's dream. Collapse of a stock market conjures up visions of stockbrokers leaping out of windows, banks closing, lenders foreclosing mortgages on penniless widows, and Okies piling their families into ancient automobiles and heading west to California from their bankrupt farms. Was it a rerun of 1929? Another Great Depression? Well, the October crash was far from heralding the start of another depression. But it contained all the elements of a disaster. Editors milked the story for all it was worth.

Television networks, the Associated Press and United Press International wire services, and news syndicate services operated by *The New York Times, The Washington Post, The Los Angeles Times* and other major newspapers filled television news shows and newspapers, big and small, with an avalanche of Wall Street reports. Big headlines! Front-page news! Television specials! Across the nation, reporters telephoned Wall Street specialists, securities house executives, stock dealers in small towns, professors of finance—anyone willing to pontificate on where the country was going. In small communities, even sportswriters were assigned to look for reaction to the gyrating markets. It was another media blitz! It won Pulitzer Prizes for two enterprising reporters! But for many Americans, Wall Street was another world, far removed from Main Street. And not one that they necessarily respected.

"It's been a nice week for the have-nots of the world," commented Ben Hamper, an assembly-line worker in the General Motors plant in Pontiac, Michigan.

In 1986 a Harris Poll survey showed that 83 percent of the people questioned believed that Wall Street operated with "unmitigated greed." Pollster Lou Harris commented that "the Eastern business establishment is a target of some antipathy in this country, and Wall Street is a symbol of that."

To check perceptions of Wall Street beyond the Hudson River, *The Wall Street Journal* placed telephone calls around the country and found out that the principal topics of conversation in the week of Black Monday were the World Series and the weather. A. C. Nielson, the company that ranks TV viewership, reported that the number of households in New York City tuned to network news on the night of Black Monday just about equaled viewing on the night of the *Challenger* space shuttle explosion. But in Chicago, professional football outperformed Wall Street about two to one, Nielson said.

What's Wall Street? "If you drew a map, it would be somewhere off the East Coast," answered Joseph Greco, a salesperson for a fastener maker in Rockford, Illinois. "It's in its own little world."

Donald Sutter, a farmer in Pleasantville, Iowa, worried because some grain, hog and cattle prices tumbled with the stocks. But his sympathy was limited. For Wall Street, he said, it was "good the way those rich people were getting hit just as us poor guys have been."

Peter Zevenbergen counsels troubled farm families from his mental health clinic in Cedar Rapids, Iowa. "When we had problems in Iowa, Wall Street told us it was because of land speculation and high debt loads," he said. "I guess we look at the Wall Street thing as the chickens come home to roost."

Dean Kocina, an official in a machinists' union in Des Plaines, Illinois, said that corporate mergers and acquisitions may have cost some Americans their jobs. "If [investors] got to be millionaires on the backs of our members, and they are no longer millionaires, I think that is wonderful," he said.

Mayor John McNamara said that machine-tool workers and farmers around his small city of Rockford, Illinois, are "people who produce things, not just paper. We try to create wealth by making things."

Richard Stavros, who owns a restaurant in Worcester, Massachusetts, also played down the economic importance of the stock market. "People have gotten away from thinking that the financial ability of this country rises and falls on Wall Street. We're the ones who keep the country going. They may keep the wheels greased, but we keep them turning."

A SCREAM: LUNCH IS LATE

Actually, the wheels were becoming ungreased on Wall Street during the week's frenetic pace. From the trading floors to the back offices, inundated with paper, Wall Street workers were putting in 14 to 16 hours a day trying to keep their heads above the markets. They got off elevators at 7 A.M. and were lucky to leave their offices by 10 P.M. or later.

Telephones never stopped ringing. Thousands of callers were put on hold—waiting, cursing, sweating, full of fear that they would lose their pants while recorded music played in their ears.

"There's no time to relax. The phones, they don't stop," commented Michael Tannucilli of Pace Securities.

Nerves were frayed. "There's a lot of people yelling at each other for insignificant stuff," said William F. Phibin of Mercator Partners. "I've seen people scream because lunch is late."

Fatigue was growing. Stanley Silverberg is a specialist on the American Stock Exchange: "I don't know how much longer I can do it. If the pace sustains itself for a few more days, the physical toll will begin to tell."

Transactions were running far too fast to handle. "It's physically beyond the capacities of the people who are on the line to effect these trades. A lot of errors are going to show up," warned Malcolm MacLean of Steifel Nicolaus and Company.

So on Thursday the New York and American Stock Exchanges announced that they would cut two hours off the schedule during the next three trading days by closing at 2 P.M. rather than 4 P.M. "The system needs time to catch its breath," John Phelan, chairman of the New York Stock Exchange, told a news conference. Both exchanges and a number of brokerage houses asked their workers to come in on the weekend and digest the mountains of paperwork left in the wake of a week that even John Pierpont Morgan could not have conceived. Several other exchanges in the United States also decided to close early for three days.

DON'T PANIC

The National Association of Securities Dealers, whose members deal in over-the-counter stocks rather than issues traded in the exchanges, sent a message this morning to the terminal screens of all its members. Big brother is watching, the Association said. The Association warned that dealers should stop trying to avoid customers who wanted to sell stock. Some dealers still were not answering their telephones.

Good news greeted the markets at today's 9:30 A.M. opening. Citibank announced that it was cutting its prime lending rate by a quarter of a percentage point, lowering it to nine percent. Other major commercial banks quickly followed suit, thus promising lower borrowing costs to businesses and consumers. Interest rates steer stock markets. Some analysts believe that Chemical Bank and Marine Midland Bank helped set off Black Monday when, in the week earlier, they increased their rates by a half point, hiking interest charges to 9¾ percent, a signal that businesses would find it more costly to borrow. If interest rates stayed up, bond investments would become more attractive than stocks because of higher yields. But no other large bank matched Chemical and Marine Midland, and, not surprisingly, they withdrew the interest increase the day after Black Monday.

This morning's cut in the prime interest rate did not help the market immediately, and Wall Street faced another torrent of sell orders when the bell opened trading. Many big financial institutions and foreign investors were dumping stocks. A decline in the prime rate should encourage buyers rather than sellers. But heavy morning selling, with buyers scarce, sent the market into dithers. Once again, a number of top-drawer companies listed on the Dow Jones Industrial Average attracted no buyers during early trading. The last of the Dow Jones stocks did not open until 11 A.M. Is it Tuesday all over again?

In an effort to head off another market collapse, the Big Board requested its members to refrain from the massive program trading that sells shares by the millions in seconds. Before noon the Dow slumped 140 points. It looked like another crash. But today's hot, heavy and volatile action suddenly eased off around noon. The Dow regained some of its strength, but closed with a loss of 77.42 points. During the day, only 361 stocks advanced in price while 1,540 shares lost value. It was the fourth-heaviest trading day in Wall Street history, 392,160,000 shares, exceeded only by the first three days of this week. The market performed nervously on Thursday, an overture to many more nervous days that would follow on Wall Street.

Would the markets ever slow down? Would prices ever stabilize? Would sanity return? At least they kept their humor. Big Board employees wore buttons that read, "Don't panic." Outside the exchange, some people held up a banner that read, "Jump."

The Horsemen of Genghis Khan
In our later-day story, the trader who had collapsed at his desk spent a night in the hospital and went home. But Wall Street was sicker than ever. Unlike 1987, no life jackets are being tossed into the market this time.

Executives in a number of corporations that could profit by buying back their own stock are postponing action. "Let's wait at least an-

other day. The way it's going, we can pick up those shares tomorrow for a couple million less."

The Federal Reserve remains silent. Bankers who handle Wall Street accounts leave for lunch two hours early, nervously reading newspapers in their clubs, and lingering long. Many bankers don't tell their secretaries where they can be reached. "I can't help Dividends Unlimited, so it's easier just not to talk with them."

No big institution tries to resuscitate a blue-chip futures index by heavy buying in its underlying stocks. "The market is too far-gone this time around to play that '87 game. I'm moving into Treasuries."

Mutual funds have been clearing out of stocks and into cash and insured short-term notes all week, deathly afraid that they face an impossible cash crunch. Small investors are telephoning at a fast rate to request immediate redemption. According to rumors on Wall Street, some mutual funds are attempting to create cash reserves as high as 75 percent on their total funds. They find it impossible to sell that many stocks, but they keep trying, loading the market with sale orders. The toll-free telephone lines into pension offices ring incessantly, and the clerks who answer know their reassurances sound hollow.

In two days of ceaseless selling, the Dow has fallen so fast that no computer system can track it. Rough estimates place the two-day loss at more than 800 points, but no one knows for sure. Trading is so heavy and the plunge so precipitous that stock tables are hopelessly outdated.

For the first time in its history, The Wall Street Journal *fails to publish price quotations for the American Stock Exchange and the over-the-counter market. Only about half the prices from the New York Stock Exchange are printed. A small article explains that most of yesterday's prices were meaningless because information systems broke down under the markets' high volatility. White spaces in stock tabulations make the financial pages in morning newspapers across the country look like checkerboards. The wire services send an editor's note to all their clients: "Due to computer delays, today's financial reports are incomplete."*

Only a few specialists attempt to open trading in their stocks. Most of these buyers of last resort have been reduced to buyers of nothing. They had exhausted their credit lines during the two previous days. Their bankers are unavailable on the telephone. Although no one can confirm the rumor, the word on Wall Street is that several specialists are trying to sell their firms to the first taker.

Rumors swirl around Wall Street like swarms of mosquitoes, biting not a few traders. For a number of years, Wall Street actually has been served by organized rumor wires. The so-called real-time news services distribute market rumors to their users along with factual reports, carefully labeling the rumors for what they are.

("If a rumor is becoming a market factor, it has to be paid heed to—there's no denying that," was the way that Desmond Maberley of Reuters explained it to The Wall Street Journal *in 1987. Other market news services also consider it their responsibility to report on significant rumors that affect trading.)*

Even before the market opens on this third day of crisis, rumors circulate that officials have agreed during an emergency breakfast meeting to close the stock exchange before it evaporates in the heat of confusion and panic. But the opening bell sounds as usual at 9:30 A.M.

A few minutes after the opening, one of the rumor wires flashes a rumor: "NYSE rumored closing before noon." A new stampede starts. Not knowing when they might be able to sell again, if at all, investors panic. They know that the lives of their institutions and their jobs depend on their ability to liquidate shares as quickly as possible and move into safer investments before trading shuts down. Once the exchange closes, who can predict when it might reopen? Or what shares might be worth when trading resumes? Sell and sell quickly—that's the only tactic left. But most buyers have vanished. The stock exchange looks like a Medieval marketplace with the horsemen of Genghis Khan approaching the gate to the city.

The trading apparatus is mortally wounded. Then suddenly the rumor is confirmed. The chairman steps forward and, as another chairman had in Hong Kong years earlier, announces that the stock exchange is hereby closed until further notice.

An hour later, our three mutual fund traders leave the stock exchange dejectedly, wondering if they would be employed tomorrow. They walk past the Italian and Chinese restaurants and head for a hotdog stand. One asks, "Either of you guys got an extra subway token?"

10

Friday, October 23

READING THE RIOT ACT

One of America's great dramas of 1987 ended today: not the saga of Wall Street, but of Robert H. Bork. By a vote of 58 to 42, the United States Senate rejected President Reagan's nomination of Judge Bork to sit on the Supreme Court. In a long confirmation hearing, Bork failed to convince enough senators that his philosophy of constitutional rights and liberties was what the country needed.

Twelve days before Black Monday, the Senate Judiciary Committee turned down the Bork nomination, nine to five. Did Bork's failure help dig the hole that Wall Street fell into? We do not believe so. But others do. Stock prices are fragile. Investors see nefarious signs in every convoluted twist and turn in human affairs. Stock prices can tumble when an explosion rips apart an oil platform in the North Sea or an airliner crashes into Mount Fuji. So, too, perhaps, when a candidate's hope for high office is dashed. Several weeks after the October crash, *The New York Times* argued that, long before the crash, Wall Street had been demonstrating confidence in Reagan's leadership despite increasing trade and budget deficits. But in blackballing Bork, the Senate committee sent a signal that the president's leadership was failing. This "added to the climate of uncertainty, deadly for financial markets," *The Times* said.

Mikhail S. Gorbachev handed the president another setback to-day. In Moscow, the Soviet leader told Secretary of State George Shultz precisely what he did not expect to hear. Shultz went to the Kremlin expecting to receive Gorbachev's proposed date for a Washington summit conference. From earlier meetings, Shultz believed the Soviets were ready. Instead, Gorbachev unexpectedly balked. Referring to Star Wars, those weapons envisioned for space warfare, the Soviet leader said, "I am put on my guard by possible results [of a summit]."

Indeed, the president's day was not pleasant. His ability to lead was being questioned. A government unsure of itself can create panic in the markets. Reagan was blaming Congress for the stock crash. "There may have been hundreds of factors affecting the uneasiness on Wall Street, but I think it's appropriate to single out some of the more likely ones," the president said.

Then he got down to brass tacks and ticked off a list of criticisms:

- Congress was considering a "dangerously protective trade bill," as it had 57 years earlier. (The Smoot-Hawley Tariff Act, passed by Congress the year after the 1929 Wall Street crash, increased import duties on such basic products as minerals, chemicals and textiles, and led more than 20 other nations to adopt retaliatory trade-protection measures. In 1932, Britain ended nearly a century of practically free trade by enacting a general tariff. Some economists view those restrictions in world trade as one of the creators of the Great Depression.)
- Congress was "unable to get control of deficit spending."
- "And there are many [in Congress] who, while refusing to cut spending, insist on increasing taxes."

Reading the riot act to Congress after the Wall Street storm, the president told delegates at a jobs conference in Washington: "Those who have to make a decision on whether or not to invest in the future of our economy see some very disturbing signs on Capitol Hill."

WAITING FOR THE DOCTOR

As the week neared its end, the Wall Street investment banker appointed by Reagan to dissect Black Monday offered a preliminary analysis of the crash in an interview with *The New York Times*.

"The principle reason for the drop was that common stocks all over the world are overvalued," said Nicholas F. Brady, chairman of the Presidential Task Force on Market Mechanisms, when *Times* financial writer Susan F. Rasky telephoned him.

In reply to Rasky's questions, the banker offered some preliminary thoughts. He spoke about the velocity and magnitude of computer stock trading that had poured selling orders onto the floor of the exchange in quantities never before seen.

"It may well be that the conclusion is that in a world of electronic and technological advances, when people come to the same conclusions all at once, you've got a lot of problems on your hands," he said. "You may need some system for slowing it all down or for helping people to understand that nothing is dramatically wrong."

Brady saw no cracks in the economy. "To me, the underlying economic conditions are fine," he said. He mentioned that government figures released today showed the U.S. economy grew by 3.8 percent in the third quarter in 1987, which ended just 19 days before Black Monday, and that inflation remained moderate.

Was the Brady commission being asked to calm public concerns about the stock market? Not precisely, he replied, but such a result would be a happy development. He offered some words of wisdom: "Calmness is built from understanding. The worst part of any sickness is the hour you spend waiting in the doctor's office thinking about how the world might end."

PANIC IS PETERING OUT

A degree of calmness descended over Wall Street today. Most shares fell in price. But the 30 blue-chip stocks that comprise the Dow Jones Industrial average inched up a fraction of a point—0.33. For the first time in a week, price volatility vanished. The roller coaster had reached its home stretch where the tracks become level. Dow Jones stock prices fluctuated within their narrowest range of the week. All week, graphs that track trading minute by minute formed a pattern of jagged spikes and deep valleys. On Friday the graph leveled to a smoother line.

"The panic is petering out," said Larry Wachtel, a market analyst with Prudential-Bache Securities.

Markets closed at 2 P.M., the first of three days with shortened trading hours. Even so, a remarkable 245.6 million shares were bought or sold on the New York Exchange during the four-and-a-half-hour session. That was the smallest total of the week, but this was a week of aberrations. Even with two hours clipped off, Friday was the tenth-busiest day in the history of the New York Stock Exchange.

"This is a relief," commented Peter G. Grennan, a stock-index analyst with Shearson Lehman Hutton. "I can't believe it. You just needed to pause. You can't think when the markets act like that."

It was for John Phelan, chairman of the Big Board, to pronounce the blessing that concluded the world's blackest financial week since 1929: "Today was the ideal script."

Humanity Would Tremble

In the ancient city of Samarkand in Central Asia, a magnificent slab of black jade, six feet long and one foot wide, marks the grave of Tamerlane, the fourteenth-century Mongol warrior. Tamerlane, which means "Timur the Lame," and his horde of horsemen left a trail of carnage when they swept across Western Asia and onto the steppes of Russia. He invaded Persia, Iraq, Armenia, Mesopotamia, Syria, Georgia, India and other lands, occupying Moscow and Delhi. One account of his bloody adventures records that "whole cities were destroyed, their populations massacred and towers built of their skulls."

Carved into the jade slab that covers his grave are the Mongol characters: "Were I alive today, humanity would tremble."

Economic forces, not warriors, can ravage the world today. Thus it was, in a later year, that people did tremble. The sudden closure of the stock exchange on Wall Street in the previous chapter's fiction created an unprecedented disruption of the capitalist system, sending shock waves throughout the world.

Shutting down the Hong Kong Stock Exchange in 1987 had been little more than a footnote to Black Monday. Hong Kong trades in companies that, while big in the colony, are minor players on the world stage. The fate of global markets is not determined by securities issued by the Bank of East Asia, China Light, Hong Kong Land, Jardine Matheson, New World Development and Swire Pacific.

But on Wall Street, blue chips rattle and shake economies around the world with the ferocity of Tamerlane 600 years ago. To many people in many countries, Wall Street is the key barometer, measuring pressures on the world's largest economy.

However the stock market is not the alpha and omega. With the exchange closed in the fictional passage, the United States still functioned. Blue-chip stocks were idle, but the companies they represented were as busy as ever. Assembly lines at General Motors continued to move. Workers at Boeing, builders of jumbo jets for flag-carriers around the globe, put together their flying machines. Exxon pumped oil, IBM experimented with a new computer system and McDonald's served another one million hamburgers.

Even so, if Wall Street fails, the world trembles. The 1929 syndrome continues to haunt. In their minds, people picture the litany of a crash: A stock market fails and then come bank closings, factory shutdowns, retail bankruptcies, unemployment, breadlines, soup kitchens and flop houses.

THE FOURTH MARKET

If Wall Street closes, investors can buy and sell securities in what is called the "fourth market." The fourth market, relatively small, operates in the shadows in America and throughout the Western world.

Although legal, the fourth market enables stocks to be traded in secrecy anyplace by anybody. Commissions and taxes can be avoided. No public records are maintained. When the regular market fails, the fourth market takes over. It is not regulated by the SEC, and it provides opportunities for manipulation. Chaos can result. The fourth market operates without disclosing any information on the prices and volume of stock trading. Transactions between investors take place, not in a central and public exchange, but privately wherever and at whatever time two or more people might decide to negotiate a stock deal.

Some fourth markets, such as the Institutional Networks Corporation (Instinet), are computerized. Instinet operates out of New York City. A computer network links Instinet to a number of terminals around the world. Subscribers enter into the computer system the name of a stock they wish to buy or sell, its bid or asked price, number of shares and a code number through which they can be contacted. This information prints out on computers of other Instinet subscribers. An interested subscriber can contact the person making the offer through the computer network and negotiate a deal. But Instinet represents the Ivy League of the fourth market. Most fourth-market activity is much less sophisticated or organized.

The exact size of the fourth market cannot be measured because its transactions are not publicly posted. In normal times, the fourth market is an insignificant force in the securities industry. Public stock exchanges work to the satisfaction of most investors. But in the aftershock of a crash, when the official exchanges are closed, the fourth market can be flooded with business.

The Little Guy

When rumors close the stock market in a future year, Little Guy is hopelessly stranded. The minute he heard rumors that the market might shut down, Little Guy called his broker and asked him to liquidate all of his modest portfolio. Along with two certificates of deposit, his shares, now falling in value, represent his life savings.

He might as well have telephoned the South Pole. The securities firm for which his broker worked was too busy trying to liquidate its own portfolio to spend time with Little Guy. Years ago, many Wall Street houses decided that their traditional business of earning commissions by trading for customers was peanuts. Big money was waiting in the roaring bull market. So investment houses put customers' accounts on the back burner and started buying and selling stocks for their own benefit. Soon their own trading became their principal business. Unable to get his broker moving, Little Guy watched helplessly while his stocks faded.

Later, he learned that even his stop-loss order had been ignored. This order instructs a specialist to sell a stock immediately after its price falls to a level that is specified in advance by the owner, thus hopefully protecting the owner against too great a loss. But Little Guy failed to read the small print. When stop orders accumulate and create a backlog of more simultaneous sales than the specialist can or wants to handle, the specialist can temporarily suspend those orders. When the specialist finally executed Little Guy's order, the price of his stock had fallen so low that he couldn't trade it in for a used lawnmower. If he had known the actual sale price, Little Guy probably would not have sold. But the transaction was out of his hands. He had filed the stop-loss order in advance, it was stalled in a backlog and, when it was finally executed, it became a runaway-loss order.

(As Professor Jack Clark Francis of Bernard M. Baruch College wrote in his 1983 textbook, Management of Investment, *"Stop orders can be suspended just at the time traders most need protection, and this somewhat diminishes their value.")*

With the market closed after its disastrous losses, organizations possessing large but deflated stock investments applied the brakes to cash flow. They attempted to hold on to their dollars a few extra days each month. They had no other choice. Their coffers were empty. Prices on their securities had fallen so low that to sell them would be tantamount to giving them away.

An insurance company delayed mailing claim checks for three or four days, hoping that no one would notice. But people did notice, and rumors spread about the company's solvency. A pension fund notified its pensioners that their monthly checks would be dated on the seventh of each month rather than the first "due to restructuring of the accounting system." Pensioners saw through that gobbledygook, and they were scared. The president of one endowed university told his faculty and staff that salary checks would be delayed one week for "administrative reasons."

A shock was delivered to investors for whom stock dividends were an important part of their income. Cash-short corporations announced that they would reduce dividend payments on their shares while maintaining the same yield. A stock's yield is computed by dividing the cash dividend by the current price of the stock. If the price of the stock declines, the yield may remain unchanged if the cash dividend is reduced.

A corporation notified its shareholders: "The dividend yield will remain the same. We have adjusted the dollar amount to reflect the current lower level of share prices."

And a retired shareholder responded: "That's crazy. What am I going to do? I need the dollars and cents for rent and food. All this talk about yields sounds like some Wall Street yuppie."

Many investors ordered their brokers to sell their stocks at any price. Said one, reflecting the views of many: "If they're cutting the dividends, I want the cash now, in my own hands." The market was losing the confidence of individual investors, large and small.

AN EARTHQUAKE AND ITS AFTERSHOCKS

The stock market crash in 1929 was only the beginning of a long decline in U.S. and world economies. Aftershocks continued until the early days of World War II. The 1930s were scarred by long-term drops in America's gross national product, collapse of banks, growing unemployment that spread to 25 percent of the population and a stock market drained of its precrash value. These economic problems were compounded by droughts, summers of relentless heat and dust storms that darkened the skies and turned America's Great Plains into the dust bowl.

Some economists believe that the Great Depression ended principally because many nations, including the United States, set out to rearm and build history's most devastating military machines. Even before the Japanese attack on Pearl Harbor in 1941, U.S. shipyards, aircraft factories and munitions plants were expanding and hiring workers to turn out military equipment for Britain as well as America's growing army and navy.

At the time of the 1929 crash, only three percent of the U.S. population was unemployed. The rate climbed sharply each year until 1933, when it stood at 25 percent, then receded slowly during Franklin D. Roosevelt's New Deal. But even in 1940, with Europe at war and the United States a year away from hostilities, 15 percent of Americans still were without jobs. Unemployment did not dip below its 1929 level until America entered the Second World War, sending virtually all able-bodied young men off to military service and putting women, such as the fabled Rosie the Riveter, into war industries.

The Dow Jones Industrial average did not recover to its precrash peak of September 29, 1929, until November 1954—25 years later. The nation's gross industrial and agricultural production remained below its pre-1929-crash level until 1940, which was the second year of the war in Europe.

In economics, the aftershocks often are worse than the earthquake, but they can be prevented.

Considering what happened in 1987, there is no doubt that financial markets urgently require fundamental changes to guard against dangerous practices. After the October 1929 stock market crash, it took Congress about three-and-a-half years, until May of 1933, to enact its first law regulating the securities industry. In today's complex computer age transactions, with markets interacting around the world, three to four years is much too long to wait for the medicine.

The Dynamics of a Disaster

In continuing our story that describes the collapse of the financial system in a later year, consider what may happen if no action is taken to change the present marketing system and if people and governments continue to make mistakes and the state of nature turns against us.

In a later year, the financial system collapses because market mechanisms around the world no longer can cope with the kind of events that occurred in 1987.

The collapse starts with a series of significant, but not disastrous, negative news developments. They are the same kind of events that had happened before—nothing new. The trade deficit is larger than forecasted, interest rates are expected to rise and the dollar is weak and is weakening. Three leading corporations among the Dow Jones Industrials announce declines in their earnings and a "temporary" reduction in dividends. Some leveraged buyouts turned sour, leaving worthless the junk bonds used to finance them. Also, several key government officials in Washington spend a weekend making statements about the "overheated economy," "overpriced stocks", "the dangerous LBO craze" and a need for the nation to buckle down, work harder and speculate less.

"Perhaps," one high official says, "what this country needs is a higher short-term capital-gains tax that can be used to reduce the national deficit and discourage speculation on the stock market."

Her view reflects the mood of the new administration in Washington. Even the president gets into the act. Addressing a convention of the Auto Workers Union, the chief executive says: "The stock market has become a big casino. This nation needs fewer gamblers and more producers." Wall Street thinks government has stabbed it in the back. News from the Middle East is bad. This time Syria is moving large military forces toward the Israeli border. Television news anchors, always searching for a dramatic angle, speak about serious threats to world peace.

The events that lead to our fictional crash are not much different from the events of 1987 described in the first nine chapters of this book. The market mechanisms that no one had bothered to fix are still creaking along. But, remembering 1987, market-makers, local and foreign investors and the general public react differently. For one thing, they demonstrate greater levels of greed and fright.

In this later year, it is not clear what triggered the initial wave of sales on Wall Street. But selling spreads along a vicious track from New York to Chicago to regional exchanges in the United States, and then leaps across the seas to cities from Tokyo to Tel Aviv. Selling envelopes all financial products: stocks, bonds, commodities, junk bonds, options, futures, indexes and different arbitrage tactics, and portfolio insurance. One slide touches off another slide. On and on it goes, straight down the mountainside.

Given the lessons of the 1987, specialists and other market-makers decide to quit early and minimize their losses. The few specialists who attempt to maintain continuity and keep the market going, as they are supposed to do, fail. Selling is too heavy, and their resources are too little, to stem the tide. At a certain point in the collapsing market, lenders cut off most credit. For everybody, the name of the game is damage control. Quit fast at any price. Cut your losses. Play the inverse of the usual rule, which is to sell high and buy low.

Remain liquid. Hold out for a lifetime opportunity to buy back at superbargain prices. Traders remember those investors who made a fortune by buying deflated stocks near the closing hour on Black Monday 1987. Sell today at any price, and buy tomorrow at lower prices. But tomorrow became an illusion. When everybody tries to sell high and buy low, no one gains.

Rumors replace credible information. The information blackout is worse than in 1987. Remembering that earlier crash, market players expect nothing. So what little information leaks through the system is rejected, because market players are in no mood to believe anything. Rumors spread. Stories abound of liquidity crises, banks that refuse to answer the phone, margin calls in the millions of dollars at noontime, dead computers and investors rushing out of mutual funds and into cash. Japanese and Europeans are selling as fast as they can, partly to cover massive losses from the free-fall in their own markets.

Says one major market player: "We went through an information vacuum in the last crash in 1987. A market without information is like a fish out of water. Based on what I know is happening now, I want out. But what I know is happening already is one hour old."

Portfolio insurance is dead. Drawing from their 1987 experiences, the big market players no longer believe in program strategies, and most certainly not during a crisis. They turn into bears, pushing prices to the ground. No energy is wasted on futures indexes, selling short, nor any of the other innovative tricks. It is back to the old-fashioned philosophy: If you are scared and don't like what's happening, you sell fast—damage control.

This time the Fed decides not to intervene nor offer a pledge for credit to overextended specialists and other traders. "The stock market should find its own equilibrium," says the newly appointed chairman, formerly an academic scholar of public finance. When he realizes that he has said the wrong thing, it is too late. The New York Stock Ex-

change already has been shut down. Actually, the exchange had been all but closed for hours before the official announcement. More than two-thirds of the stocks were not trading, many did not even open, others went through long delays in opening. Large bid-to-ask spreads made trading prohibitive. Market indexes were meaningless, the computer system failed, clearing opportunities halted and other mistakes, deliberate or otherwise, mounted by the minute. Nobody trusted anybody.

When stock markets close in New York and other U.S. cities, the derivative markets in Chicago fall silent. But the fourth market flourishes under a variety of names: "curb market" or "under-the-counter market" or, borrowing the British term, the "gray market." Some fourth-market activity passes through computers. But most of this private trading is conducted person to person as in a traditional Persian market, but without all the Eastern color.

The fourth market operates in fancy corporate board rooms, in crowded computer rooms, in the dark corners of parking garages and in bars. Some deals are even struck outdoors under the trees, just as in George Washington's day. Desperate people try to sell stock certificates for cash to people who are trying to get something for next to nothing. Instead of one large coordinated market, thousands of small scattered trading places emerge with broad differences in price for the same security at any given time. No continuous trading. No real competition. No controls. No information. No records, and a lot of manipulation, fear and panic.

Large corporations decide to postpone their buybacks in hopes of even lower prices. This time, they won't even announce buybacks. It is a meaningless decision. They lack liquid resources to purchase any stocks, and they need to conserve every dollar as survival resources in the mounting crisis. Even if they possess cash, they can't start buyback activities. The markets that handle mass transactions are closed.

News from abroad is just as bad, if not worse. Security markets are closing their shutters around the world. Financiers are fleeing from international investments into domestic bomb shelters built from their own government's notes, cash or gold—mainly gold. Fear, rumors and liquidity crises envelop the trading world.

Does anyone try to manipulate a small futures market index like the MMI to push up its price and reverse the downward trend to save the market? No. Not this time. New rules on insider trading and anticollaboration plus the mood of the public against any kind of market interference eliminate the slightest thought of index manipulation. The big-money folks are afraid to risk it. Besides, who wants to touch the futures market in a crisis like this? Memories remain fresh. All markets handling futures indexes, except one, had closed on Tuesday, October 20, 1987, the day after Black Monday. A closed futures index is worse than a closed stock. The lifespan of a futures index is dated. "It could die on you," one trader said.

Thus, factors that saved the system in 1987 do not work this time. The Fed is less generous. The Hong Kong syndrome takes over, and markets are suspended. Nothing activates the MMI or any other futures index. No corporate buybacks. And this time, the bargain hunters, the deep-water anglers, are too frightened and too greedy. They want waters real deep, prices at their lowest possible levels. The dynamics of the black hole lead to a big bang.

In Washington, government officials and later the Fed issue encouraging statements about the "strong economy," the "solid fundamentals," and the "peaceful world." It is nonsense. No one believes the intended reassurances. The capitalist financial market mechanisms have collapsed, not the economy. The water is healthy. But the pipeline system through which markets flow does not work. The pipes are inadequate, old, rusted and leaking. They cannot withstand the market pressures. Nor can the pipes be repaired quickly. And, under chaotic crisis conditions, the economic pipelines most certainly cannot be fixed by the usual Keynesian remedies of government intervention in the marketplace.

In this future crash, a number of important banks suffer heavy losses on leverage buyout transactions, junk bonds and on loans secured by stocks that have plummeted in value. At the same time, several developing nations in South America and Asia waste billions of dollars building factories that produce reasonably good products. Unfortunately, the same or better products can be purchased cheaper from another country. A portion of the billions of dollars help build a new presidential palace and strengthen military forces loyal to its occupant. The problem is that the billions came from loans granted by American banks.

In normal times, the U.S. banking system could cope with shaky Third World loans. But banks lose heavily in defaulted loans to the securities industry, in risky leveraged buyouts and junk bonds that banks purchased in the billions of dollars, and then on loans to nations around the world. They find themselves in more trouble than they were in 1933, when President Roosevelt declared a bank holiday and 3,460 banks failed to reopen after the holiday ended.

Black Monday in 1987 did not cause any immediate bank closures. But the resources of a number of banks were strained in the 1987 crash, and many of them were technically bankrupt in 1988, saved only by creative accounting.

The tariff wars that wrecked international trade in the 1930s were not refought. In 1929 the United States enjoyed an international trade surplus of $1.1 billion. In an effort to enrichen this surplus by protecting American manufacturers and farmers from foreign imports, Congress in 1930 enacted the Smoot-Hawley tariff bill. Foreign governments retaliated with their own high tariff barriers, and international trade fell sharply. Within three years, the U.S. trade surplus had dropped to $400 million.

In this future year, Washington is determined not to make that mistake again. But the nations of the world have developed techniques more subtle than tariffs in their attempts to swing international trade in their favor. They maintain undervalued currencies so their products will sell at bargain prices abroad. They subsidize exports by charging high prices at home, and dumping prices abroad. They design inspection procedures and "quality" standards that make it virtually impossible for a foreign article to be approved for sale. Or they establish inspection rules with red tape so complicated and time-consuming as to discourage importers. Or they maintain merchandise distribution systems that foreigners cannot penetrate. The greenback falls out of control, sharply increasing the prices of imports into the United States and thus triggering inflation. So even without the high tariff barriers of the 1930s, international trade becomes a battleground, rocking capital markets and shattering international cooperation.

When a container no longer can hold a substance, you lose that substance. Once the initial market crisis started, wave after wave of aftershocks roll across the financial markets of the world. The aftershocks become a self-sustained cycle of falling confidence, falling prices, liquidity crises, information deficiencies, massive losses generating still-lower levels of confidence, and on and on, like a perpetual-motion machine, accelerating its speed until it flies apart in a million pieces.

It can happen.

On December 20, 1987, *The Wall Street Journal* said: "Tuesday [October 20, the day after Black Monday] was the most dangerous day we have had in 50 years."

The General Accounting Office, the congressional watchdog, said: "Had the precipitous decline continued for even another day, massive disruptions to the United States financial system might have occurred."

The Securities and Exchange Commission said: "We note that the October market break did not result in merely a dramatic one-time reevaluation of securities markets. The aftershocks of October 19 continue to affect the market today."

The Presidential Task Force said: "It was midday Tuesday that the securities markets and the financial system approached breakdown."

11

After the Crash

THE SECOND SPECULATIVE BUBBLE

Leveraged buyouts, corporate takeovers and junk bonds turned the postcrash period into a dangerous game of adventure capitalism. Wheeler-dealers perfected the art of using other people's money to make themselves billionaires. Hostile raiders bought companies as if they were pieces of real estate in a Monopoly game and changed, probably forever, the capital markets of the Western world. Corporate raiders, often with little starting capital, introduced new dimensions of speculation unheard of since the Dutch tulip craze of the seventeenth century. Around 1637, in the Low Countries, extraordinary speculation in tulips resulted in a craze that was called "tulipomania." Prices for single roots rose as high as 2,600 guilders ($1,290 in January 1989 dollars). When the bubble burst, thousands of people were left bankrupt, holding only tulips.

The 1987 stock market crash was followed by big and bold raids on corporations large and small, among them some of the largest companies in America. Speculators swept up stock in quantities vast enough to steal companies from their boards of directors. Mergers and acquisitions became a fact of corporate life, and much of the action involved unfriendly takeovers of corporations by capitalistic buccaneers. Call them sharks; they outdid the robber barons of the nineteenth century. In 1976, there were about 1,100 mergers and takeovers of companies valued at $1 million or more. In 1987, that figure jumped to 3,700. Corporate takeovers dominated the financial world after the 1987 crash. Estimates varied on how much money changed hands in mergers and acquisitions during 1988, ranging from $216 billion to $453 billion. Whatever the figure, the lessons of Black Monday were forgotten, and a new speculative craze attracted the wits and resources of the big money guys: banks, financial institutions and lone rangers.

Deal-makers discovered that many corporations were undervalued on Wall Street. The assets and the present value of future earnings of such companies were worth more than the market value of their total outstanding stock. An acquisition shark could clean up by dismantling a corporation and selling off some of its operating divisions or even such straight assets as real estate, worth its area in gold. Sharks needed almost no cash of their own to initiate a deal. They borrowed money by issuing junk bonds, so-called because their credit ratings are low. But to offset the risk, junk bonds pay high yields. In the late 1980s, they became attractive investments for banks, insurance companies, pension and mutual funds, savings and loan associations, and other financial institutions looking for high yields on their investments.

Savings and loan banks, in which Main Street Americans had deposited their money and financed their home mortgages for generations, certainly could not afford to take any more risks. S&Ls were in their worst shape since the Great Depression. In 1988, federal regulators rescued or closed 217 insolvent savings institutions—the highest number since 1938—at a cost of $38 billion. On January 2, 1989, *The New York Times* estimated that one-third of all savings institutions in the United States were insolvent.

Corporate raiders began stalking cash cows, businesses which generate a rich flow of cash and possess assets that exceed the market price of their stock. The takeover artist sells junk bonds and uses the proceeds to accumulate stock in a target company by offering to buy its shares at a price above what they are trading for on Wall Street. The successful shark rakes in sufficient stock to gain control of the company, then pays off the junk bonds from the company's earnings and/or by selling off some of the business' assets or its operating branches. The raider is using debt in the form of bonds to burrow into a corporation, a tactic known as a leveraged buyout (LBO). Properly tuned, an LBO can be highly profitable. Interest paid on junk bonds is tax-deductible, while dividends paid to stock-holders are not. Thus, by turning equity (stocks) into debt (junk bonds), corporate raiders earn a significant tax break by reducing the taxable cash dividends paid to stockholders. Turning junk bonds into corporate ownership is the twentieth century model of medieval alchemy, a chemistry that attempted to transform base metals into gold. Through tax breaks, Wall Street's modern alchemy is subsidized by the government, using taxpayers' money.

Alchemy never worked. But after the 1987 Wall Street crash, financial alchemy performed miracles—or so it seemed at the beginning. As easily as water turns into ice at the North Pole, the paper on which LBOs are written metamorphosed into gold. Accelerating into high gear during the postcrash period, the value of junk bonds reached $130 billion just before the 1987 stock market crash, and a large share of them were financing LBO deals. After the market crisis, junk bonds grew even faster and became the major force dominating financial markets. At the end of 1988, *The New York Times* estimated the total face value of high-yielding bonds at $180 billion, and even more money was waiting in the wings to finance future LBOs. *The Times* put the amount of equity funds available in 1988 for future leveraged buyouts at nearly $25 billion. Since $1 of equity typically can support $10 worth of debt, Wall Street could finance another $250 billion in LBOs, *The Times* said.

These billions of dollars proliferated into staggering corporate takeovers. Academics in their ivory towers and traders on Wall Street agreed in the postcrash period that no company, large or small, was safe from the hostile axes of fast-dollar company choppers. Sharks were poised to pounce on many more firms and sell off their parts for profits that would produce economic empires for the raiders. Sometimes a raider left the target corporation in ashes. Several years ago, one of the authors of this book saw the new owners of his company, United Press International, sell off the firm's only profitable products before seeking protection from creditors under Chapter 11 of the Federal Bankruptcy code.

The takeover LBO-junk bond fever spread across the oceans and became a world game. European, Australian and Japanese investors started buying America—American companies, that is—and they also helped finance domestic LBOs in the United States. In the first six months of 1988, foreign investors spent $15.5 billion in hostile takeovers of American companies, the U.S. Congress' General Accounting Office reported. Foreign investors paid an additional $4.7 billion in friendly takeovers. During that same period, Americans spent $68.7 billion in acquiring American companies. It is estimated that about nine percent of all U.S. bank loans to corporate customers in 1987 involved leveraged buyouts. In several large transactions, Japanese banks financed as much as 30 percent of an LBO loan in the United States.

The junk-bond takeover game hit jackpots in 1988 that would have impressed even John D. Rockefeller or John Pierpont Morgan.

- In the biggest corporate purchase in history, nearly twice the size of any previous takeover, Kohlberg Kravis Roberts & Company executed a $25.07-billion leveraged buyout of RJR Nabisco, a cash cow festooned with gilt edges. Its consumer products ring bells at supermarkets around the world, any one of which could be sold for a king's ransom: Del Monte fruits and vegetables, Oreo cookies, Planters nuts, Life Savers, Ritz crackers, Winston, Salem, and Camel cigarettes. RJR Nabisco's cigarettes and cookies alone generate an annual cash flow of $2.4 billion.
- On December 21, 1988, less than a month after the RJR Nabisco takeover, Drexel Burnham Lambert, Inc., agreed to pay a record $650 million in fines and restitution rather than face prosecution for securities crimes. Drexel Burnham was the lead junk-bond underwriter involved in the grab for RJR Nabisco and many previous deals. Living far from Wall Street in a Beverly Hills, California, house once occupied by movie greats Clark Gable and Carole Lombard, financial wizard Michael R. Milken, 42, had converted Drexel Burnham into the world's leading junk-bond dealer. Milken's studies at the University of California in Berkeley during the 1960s, and later as a graduate business student at Pennsylvania's Wharton School, convinced him that big bucks could be earned peddling high-risk, high-yield bonds. He proved his thesis at Drexel Burnham, which had been a relatively small securities house on Wall Street before Milken's arrival. He shifted the firm's junk-bond desk from Wall Street to his native California and built junk bonds into the powerful engine that drove the boom in mergers and acquisitions through the 1980s. By 1988, an estimated 90 percent of Drexel's revenues was coming from takeover financing. The firm earned $522 million in 1986, and Milken's bonuses have been estimated to be as high as $200 million a year.

During 1988, a record of about $96 billion was withdrawn from stocks in the United States, mostly to finance corporate takeovers and restructuring, *The Wall Street Journal* reported at the end of the year.

In addition to RJR Nabisco, there were other big-buck takeovers in 1988:

- Kraft was bought by Philip Morris for $13.4 billion.
- Federated Department Stores was bought by Campeau Corporation of Canada for $7.4 billion.
- Pillsbury was bought by Grand Metropolitan PLC, a British conglomerate, for $5.7 billion.
- Farmers Insurance Group was bought by Batus Industries of Britain for $5.3 billion.
- Sterling Drug was bought by Eastman Kodak for $5.1 billion.
- Montgomery Ward was acquired from Mobil Corporation in a management-led LBO for $3.8 billion.
- Hospital Corporation of America was acquired by its management for $3.6 billion.
- Fort Howard Paper Corporation was acquired in a management LBO for $3.6 billion.
- Triangle Publications, publisher of TV Guide, was bought by media mogul Rupert Murdoch of Australia for $3 billion.

Like RJR Nabisco, many of the takeover targets were companies involved in manufacturing, distributing and selling of mass-market consumer goods that promised to be cash cows for generations to come. But in a year in which Christian evangelism became entangled in sex, mansions, money and a Christian theme park, even the Word of God was taken over. Stephen Mernick, an orthodox Jew and Toronto real estate developer, acquired for $65 million the assets of the bankrupt PTL Ministries once run by the television preacher Jim Bakker and his wife Tammy.

LBO transactions appeared to offer prizes to all the players. The big financial institutions that control more than 80 percent of all stock trading loved and encouraged LBOs. For at least five reasons, they viewed LBOs as a win-win situation with nothing to lose.

As equity portfolio managers, their mouths watered at the sight of the premiums offered by corporate raiders who wanted to buy their stocks. As investment bankers, the fees paid to them for organizing buyouts and floating junk bonds were astronomical, even by the scales that weigh Wall Street. For example, in the RJR Nabisco whopper, financial advisory fees reached $202 million for Drexel and $84 million for Merrill Lynch. As institutional nonequity funds managers, they enhanced the performance of their portfolios by shifting funds into junk bonds with high yields, instead of relying solely on high-grade bonds that indeed are safer but yield poorly. Furthermore, as traders, they were overjoyed by the frequent postcrash market rallies on Wall Street that were triggered by take-over activities. And, lastly, as managers of mutual funds, they were exhilarated by the challenge of dealing in an exciting new financial product, LBO mutual funds.

What about risk? With Black Monday all but forgotten, portfolio managers dealing in LBO stocks and junk bonds considered themselves safe so long as they diversified and demonstrated a high degree of financial creativity. After all, Michael Milkin proved that point in a term paper that he wrote at the Wharton School. His studies completed, he put his theories of creative finance into practice and amassed a personal fortune estimated to total at least $500 million.

Once again, greed took over on Wall Street. But the greed mania touched only the big money guys. Small investors sat frightened on the market sidelines and watched the dinosaurs battle.

A Bad Day at Items Galore

But on a future date, disaster strikes. The deal-makers forgot that it is impossible to get something for nothing day after day. Even on Wall Street, alchemy does not work. While it sounds unbeatable on paper, the LBO/junk bond strategy requires almost perfect soil, fertilizer and growing weather. The success of any LBO transaction depends on a number of critical conditions. A buyer must be found to purchase some of the assets of the acquired company, and/or the firm that is taken over must generate enough cash flow to pay off the junk loans.

With LBOs, junk bonds, bridge loans, bluff, blunder and gall, the Wall Street firm of Rigger Raiders pulls off a hostile takeover of Items Galore, a vast conglomerate that manufactures consumer goods for all ages, from disposable diapers to coffins, and for all sexes, from lip-sticks to jockstraps. But to its horror, Rigger Raiders can find no buy-ers for the crown jewels of Items Galore, its corporate divisions that had been generating bountiful cash flows. Times are changing in such a way as to erode the future prospects of some of the most profitable merchandise lines handled by Items Galore. The birthrate is falling, and so, in the minds of potential corporate buyers, diapers lack long-range growth. The popularity of cremations is increasing, depressing coffins. Lipsticks skid at the mercy of a new teenage fad, The Natural Look. Athletic supporters slip when a paperback book hits the best-seller list with an alarming title: Jogging Can Be Dangerous to Your Health. True or not, that is how potential buyers perceive the future. They simply are not interested in a company that manufactures products whose time had ended.

Then the unexpected happens. Rigger's aggressive effort to sell off parts of Items Galore backfires, because the employees don't trust these new wheeler-dealers. Middle managers and factory workers see their jobs being sacrificed by fast-buck deal-makers who are out to make an overnight killing rather than planning for the company's long-term growth. Rumors swirl through Items Galore's offices and plants. Employees linger longer at coffee breaks to collect corporate gossip. They worry if their jobs are safe, given Rigger Raider's hit-and-run tactics. Their minds preoccupied with nightmares of an uncertain future, workers stumble and fumble and production suffers. Many of them feel that they are being treated unfairly. Rigger's corporate greed rubs off on the hired hands, and they look for a piece of the action before it's too late.

"I heard on the evening news last night that the new owners shelled out 22 billion bucks for this company," Diaper Padder said, stirring her second cup of coffee. "They ought to be able to add a couple of bucks to the seven-fifty I'm making an hour."

"Jeez," replied Bottom Fastener. "You making seven-fifty? I'm still at seven-twenty. I'll settle for a flat ten dollars out of those billions."

"Truth is, we'll be lucky to hold onto our jobs. I heard on the bus coming in this morning that Rigger Raiders may sell the diaper division to Three Pees—that's Perfect Paper Products. That company makes diapers so they fold instead of fasten, and they've come out with a new superabsorbent synthetic polymer that cuts down on the padding."

"Jesus, that sounds bad for our diapers. You going back to the line?"

"Nah. Think I'll have another coffee. It's about time for lunch anyhow. Besides, what am I doing padding diapers for Mr. Big Bucks while waiting for Three Pees to hand out the pink slips?"

Gripes and rumors fuel more gripes and rumors, spreading through all divisions of Items Galore. Factory workers, clerks, secre-

taries, accountants, salespeople, janitors, chemists, engineers and all the other people who make a company great lie awake at night, fearful of what Rigger Raiders—total outsiders—will do to their old and honored company, and its trademarks that have been household names since before grandfather's day, trademarks that are a part of America's heritage.

Company loyalty from employees has its place. But with Rigger Raider already sitting in their front parlor, the main concern of most workers is for their own pocketbook. Union leaders, who were perceived by their members as being too soft with the old owners, see a once-in-a-lifetime opportunity. By disrupting production at the very moment that the new management is trying to milk the firm of assets and cash, the union stands a good chance of winning important concessions and strengthening the loyalty of its members. Strikes are called to demand job security and raises. Pickets chant for higher wages: "You've got billions. We've got bills."

Middle managers in Items Galore, at least the ones who know that they are good at what they do, look around for new jobs. Many of them leave Items Galore. Among those who remain, morale dips, dragging down productivity and earnings even more.

For Rigger Raiders, the LBO equation is not working. Their cash cow shrivels before their eyes. Greed blinded them. They are unable either to run the corporation profitably or to sell off its parts. Beset by labor unrest, low morale acquired and overstocked on products with a declining market, Items Galore loses its luster. The Wall Street Journal *writes an article that exposes several juicy but unsavory aspects of the takeover tactics of Rigger Raiders. Mounting uncertainty wrought by the hostile takeover and a bad press turn employees into careless workers. Mistakes are made on the assembly line, on the shipping docks, in the billing departments and in order-processing. Product quality suffers. Sales decline. Profits sag. The cash flow that Rigger Raiders needs—to pay the mounting interest on its junk bonds and to meet early maturity issues—slows to a cash trickle.*

The company takes its only option. To stave off creditors, it seeks protection in Chapter 11 of the Bankruptcy Code. The high yields promised by its junk bonds vanish in the night and, like Cinderella, the golden bond reverts to paper. Several savings and loan associations, a large bank and a medium-sized insurance company are left holding junk securities with no more value than the loans made by U.S. banks to Third World nations. Several pension funds, signifi-

cantly invested in LBO financing, withhold payments to the old folks. The financial world is shocked.

The LBO failure at Items Galore colors other corporations. Assets offered for sale by other recent corporate takeovers go begging. Potential buyers wait, figuring that the price asked for those assets must and will decline. "Don't purchase real estate just as the enemy starts to break through the city gates," says one investor.

When one major LBO fails, the future of all high-yield debt dims, and the junk bond market collapses. To make matters even worse, value drains out of the traditional, low-yield "investment-grade" bonds. Because high-yield bonds have invaded and diluted the corporate capital structure, "investment-grade" bonds become less secure. Consequently, their prices fall and their yields climb, and they become junk bonds themselves. In many cases, their market value is reduced by more than half. Financial difficulties follow, critically weakening most financial institutions—not only those heavily invested in junk bonds, but also institutions invested in "investment-grade" bonds.

The bond crisis hits banks, pension funds, insurance companies, mutual funds, and hundreds of relatively small savings and loan associations, on Main Streets across America, that had been struggling for years to stave off insolvency. The kiss of death is planted on their ledgers. This time, the Federal Reserve and other government agencies refuse to help as they did in the past. From the start, the Fed and regulatory agencies had warned against the junk-bond fever. This time they allow the fever to claim its victims. Last but not least, the innocent target companies in the LBO game suffer the most. Many go bankrupt. And what happens to the asset-strippers who started the mess in the first place? Their investments crumble. But, ironically, the buyout dealers suffer less than anyone. They were using other people's money.

Yet another irony is played out, this one in the ivy-covered walls of academe. Several finance professors do some fast dancing when the LBOs come tumbling down. At one time in academic and professional journals, they were touting the "unique virtue of junk bonds that, when widely diversified, carry high return and low risk." Now they publish new papers stating that diversification will not work under crisis situations because the "specific risk is substituted by systematic risk and systematic risk is undiversifiable."

It's the same old story played over again, just like the perils of portfolio insurance that insures stocks except when insurance is needed the most—when the market is crashing.

Thus, what seemed to be an all-win situation becomes instead a national financial disaster. Individual investors are turned off by the takeover war between corporate dinosaurs. LBOs, junk bonds and potential new Black Mondays scare them off Wall Street. Wall Street looks more and more like a high-stakes gambling den, rather than a marketplace for savings and investing in the future of corporate America. Wall Street frightens individual investors. They do not understand the game any more. Many investors desert the market and move their funds into a safe haven, U.S. Treasury bills.

"We were lucky," says the investment banker to his friend on the commuter train back to Long Island after their longest day in the office.

"Lucky?"

"Sure. Imagine where we would have landed if we were in the midst of a recession or just an economic slowdown."

"You call that luck? Just about as lucky as the guy on death row who wins a stay of execution."

THE TAKEOVER MASTER: WORSE THAN BLACK MONDAY

What will happen to the stock market when the huge takeover/LBO/junk-bond business fails, combined with the other weaknesses in the market system discussed in earlier chapters? Complete disaster!

Harold S. Geneen, the former chief executive of ITT, one of the world's largest corporations, became a master of mergers and acquisitions, buying up more than 350 companies and folding them into ITT. It is estimated that he paid about $6 billion for companies that had grown in worth to around $15 billion by 1988. But Geneen was a B-LBO man—before leverage buyouts. He collected companies in the old-fashioned way with equity money, not junk bonds, and he bought companies for their long-term growth, not an overnight profit.

In an interview with *Forbes* magazine near the end of 1988, Geneen compared leveraged takeover sharks to car thieves. "There are people who go out stealing Mercedes cars," he told the magazine. "They chop them up and sell the parts because, according to price lists, they can get more for the parts than for the assembled car. There's something wrong when the parts are worth more than the assembled car, but that's the way the system works—on Wall Street, too."

Chop and sell is one of the rubrics in the theology of LBOs. But there is a problem. Except, perhaps, in the luxury car business, few products sell at list price, particularly during times of growing uncertainty. And, most important for LBOs, who can say what is the list price of a company or its components?

Decent American companies located far from Wall Street can be destroyed or corrupted by hostile takeovers or by the mere threat of takeover. To defend themselves against raiding sharks, corporations sometimes have no choice but to adopt what Wall Street calls the scorched-earth policy: selling off the most attractive parts of their business, their crown jewels, and/or scheduling new debt. Either step will diminish a target company's appeal to a raider. The firm sells off pieces of its business and distributes the proceeds to stockholders. Or so-called "Poison Pill" techniques are used. The company borrows money, creating large new debt that would overburden the raider and hopefully frighten him back into his lair. The target company then distributes its borrowed funds to stockholders in the form of special dividends.

"You see companies that follow this scorched-earth process," said Geneen, the master acquirer. "They go out and borrow as much as they can and give it to the stockholders. So, there's no reason to take the company over because [management] has already burned the place down. By the way, these aren't bastards doing this. They don't have a choice."

But sadly, the scorched-earth defense policy against a takeover, while it can drive the shark out to sea, may be just as bad as handing the business over to the raider in the first place. Scorching the corporate earth is like chopping up your furniture to feed the fireplace. Either the successful raider strips the acquired company of its jewels, or management strips the assets to defend against a raid. Either way, production capacity declines, long-term investments are deferred, research and development is shunted aside, capital is consumed rather than invested, and companies borrow to their ears, committing income to interest payments.

Everybody across the land can be critically affected by the dangerous LBO game: those who are directly and indirectly involved in a takeover, and those who are not involved but are terrorized by the threat. When the final test of takeover junk-bond financing is taken, the price can be high: decline in competitiveness as companies merge, inflation as monopolies increase prices, failure of financial institutions as bonds shed their worth, and unemployment and bankruptcies as the economy degenerates. What at the start looked like creative, no-loss innovative finance turns into another Dutch tulip bubble.

Unfortunately, dangers created by the speculation that followed the 1987 crash do not threaten only the few speculative investors who can afford the risk. The financial instruments used in leveraged buyouts are bought and held by a broad base of banks, savings and loans, insurance companies, pension funds and other institutional investors who are supposed to avoid risk.

"A lot of this paper is not very well-seasoned—it's never been through a recession," Geneen told *Forbes* writer Subrata N. Chakravarty. "In a time of major recession, it will sweep both direct and indirect interests. The acceleration this would add to a recession would be substantial. October 19 [1987] would be small compared to these possibilities."

We could not agree more.

Epilogue: Ticking Like a Time Bomb

MONKS IN THE CHURCH OF CAPITALISM

Seldom do big disasters strike without a warning. Pain flashes through the human body when a major organ starts to falter. Financial reports scream, or at least shout, before a company reaches bankruptcy. Noises develop in the engine or around the chassis before a car fails. Hurricanes in the Atlantic and typhoons in the Pacific are generated at sea where radar tracks their movements before they strike land. Corruption, waste and shaky leadership signal a decaying political regime.

And so it is with economic systems. Warning bells ring before a financial disaster. Consider, for example, the Great Depression. The Wall Street crash of 1929 accounted for only one-fifth of the stock market loss that led into the bleak years of the 1930s. After 1929, the market continued to decline for two years until it reached its bottom. Through the same long period, America's gross national product and its employment slid slowly into the valley of despair while the warning bells were sounding. And then it took 25 years, until November 1954, through World War II and the Korean War, before the Dow Jones Industrial Average regained and passed its 1929 pre-crash peak.

The 1929 crash was an early warning signal. That signal packed a tremendous blow. But neither government nor business took any effective steps to deal with the 1929 problems until it was too late. For its inaction, the nation, and the world, paid a tremendous price: the Great Depression.

If early warnings are taken seriously, a crisis oftentimes can be prevented. Like the bell that clangs while the fire-station doors open, the crash of October 1987 sounded a deafening alarm. But 18 months later no fire engines had left the firehouses. And no one seems to have heard the alarm. The factors that caused the crash still were gnawing on national and international financial systems in 1989, and their intensity was being magnified. Yet neither the investment industry nor governments had moved to put their houses in order.

When this book was written, confidence in the market was lower than it was during the bull days before Black Monday. Investors were nervous. They had seen the crash, and they would never forget. Interest rates were high and so were the twin deficits: the national budget and the U.S. trade balance. The dollar was not much stronger. Faith in the idea that government intervention could protect U.S. currency from foreign onslaughts had diminished.

After the 1987 crash, international markets became trickier and more complicated than ever before. A case in point is the Tokyo Stock Exchange. In 1988, for the first time, Tokyo started trading in index futures, one of the active ingredients in the U.S. stock market crash a year earlier. The Tokyo exchange was the largest stock market in the world even before it launched futures in September 1988. While influencing U.S. capital markets in significant ways, the Tokyo exchange operates differently than Wall Street and, of course, carries on its transactions outside American regulatory systems. But, at its own pace, Japan's capital market has been following New York and Chicago into the complexities of the creative finance that can trigger another crisis.

In 1989, Tokyo is scheduled to open an options market and is expected to offer even more complex financial products. There is little doubt that program trading itself eventually will be introduced into Japan. With world markets becoming more interdependent than ever before, index trading in Japan is bound to affect operations in other world markets and make domestic regulatory measures in the United States less effective.

The dynamics of the learning process cannot be ignored. Market participants learned their lessons in 1987. At the outset of the next crisis, they may react more swiftly and in more extreme ways to save their own necks. Specialists and other market-makers may throw in the towel earlier, close their shops and bring orderly trading to a roaring halt.

The entire financial system is far more vulnerable now than it was before Black Monday: A second heart attack usually is more severe than the first.

With only two exceptions, no prescriptions were written to cure the markets during the first 18 months after the 1987 crash. Federal regulators announced on October 18, 1988, that circuit breakers, a controversial market device, would be tested for one year. The breakers provide for a one-hour trading halt when the Dow Jones average drops 250 points or more from the previous day's closing and a two-hour halt if the Dow falls by 400 points. Minor changes were made in margin requirements on the Chicago Mercantile Exchange. But these alterations fell far short of dealing with the multitude of problems plaguing the market system.

At least four major committees and task forces and hundreds of independent experts did an excellent job in collecting the evidence left by the crash, assessing what went wrong, and making recommendations on how to fix the system. While the experts do not all agree on the details, one conclusion is clear: Critical problems exist in the way in which financial systems work, and these problems should be dealt with promptly. When the warning bell sounded in 1987, few listened and little was done. At best, it would be naive, if not downright irresponsible, to assume that the October 1987 crash was a one-time-only event.

In Biblical days, when men, women and systems failed, the prophets played an important role. They stood near the main gate of the town, where many people passed, and spoke out on the problems of the day, emphasizing what was going wrong, describing the consequences and calling for changes. To be heard, the prophets recited poems, proverbs, allegories and stories. Paradoxically, they made bad news sound almost enjoyable.

Today, academics and journalists sometimes play the role of monks in the church of capitalism. Fortunately, we do not have to stand at the gate to the town. But, concerned about the dangers disclosed in the 1987 crash, we—a professor and a journalist—used our word processors to present facts, proverbs, allegories and stories that describe the era of Black Monday. In this book we describe disastrous events that almost happened and that could happen in the future. We pushed these events to the extreme to present a *worst-case scenario*. But we tried not to push too far. Look again. Compare the factual accounts in this book with the fictional sections. They may not be too far apart. The fiction can happen. Even if the probability is small that our fiction will become fact, precautionary measures must be taken, just as with the threat of a nuclear meltdown, to avoid catastrophic consequences.

The faults that we describe in this book can be corrected. Fortunately, the country faced no severe economic problems during the period that followed the crash. The foundations of our economy generally were stable. But the financial mechanisms of the world need fixing. Otherwise, another crash could create a chain of events around the world that would lead to a crisis far beyond the underlying economic problems themselves. Interaction between financial markets and national and international economies is much stronger today than ever before in the past.

The 1987 crash demonstrated that the mechanisms of the market system are suffering from a severe case of old age. The volume of trading today and its worldwide scope are more than the old skeleton can prop up and carry. For most of the last 50 years, the system worked fine. But Black Monday and its aftermath broke pivotal bones. The old skeleton may collapse unless it undergoes major surgery and general rejuvenation.

What needs fixing? A summary of what went wrong in October 1987 tells us what needs fixing. Here is our list:

- Market-making collapsed on both the securities and futures markets. Critical weaknesses developed in dealing with order imbalances when sellers significantly outnumbered buyers and vice versa. The inability to clear the market in an orderly and continuous fashion resulted in delays in openings, extreme price volatility, trading halts, accumulation of unexecuted orders and general confusion. These failures raised the alarming possibility that markets would be closed. The specialist system that is critical to the trading mechanism as it is now structured came close to complete collapse. "The trading system was not working well," the General Accounting Office said cautiously.
- Financial assets of the specialists, the buyers of last resort, were inadequate to handle the crisis.

- During the crash, off-floor transactions by the big upstairs firms stopped often, leaving specialists naked on the floor to fight an impossible battle against crashing prices. The upstairs firms did not provide the anticipated liquidity.
- While the evidence is unclear, relations between investment houses and specialists should be questioned. To prevent possible price manipulations, these relationships should be monitored closely and regulated.
- Many market-makers in the over-the-counter market withdrew completely from the battlefield. Markets for their securities ceased to exist.
- Information systems on individual stocks and market indexes collapsed into misinformation, confusion and a loss of trust. Opening delays, trading halts and computer failure made it impossible at times to determine transaction prices and calculate meaningful market indexes. During the crash, the information system degenerated to such a point that at times traders could not even determine whether the market was falling or climbing.
- Inadequate computer capacity led to a breakdown in the DOT system, delays in executing orders, tardy market statistics and outright mistakes.
- The clearing system through which cash shifts from buyer to seller blocked up, seriously delaying movement of millions of dollars between brokers, customers, exchanges and banks.
- Limit orders to buy or sell a stock at a specific price or better, a tool that is critical in protecting investors during a volatile market, failed to work because timely information on order execution was scarce and the computerized DOT system was closed. Many limit orders never were executed. Compounding the problem, many investors never learned that their orders had been ignored until it was too late to safeguard their investments.
- Money market funds had become a major liquid saving instrument. But many of these funds were operating outside banking regulations, often by companies involved in high-risk market transactions.
- A lot of investors, particularly the small ones, were unable to reach their brokers during the crisis. For many investors, brokers had become their bankers by investing in short-term money-market instruments and by advancing loans against stocks. But

investors lost control of their funds because their brokers' telephones were constantly busy or never answered.

- Thousands of small investors complained that their brokers conducted unauthorized trading for them or provided misleading information and wrong advice. Two-thirds of the small investors who complained about their brokers in 1987 still were waiting for answers a year later, the North American Securities Administrators Association reported.

- To an extreme, trading activity was concentrated in a small number of big investors. They dominated both stock and futures markets. During the crash, small investors were unable to obtain equal access to trading opportunities. Large sums of money could be lost in a few minutes. But the little guy lacked the financial clout to be given speedy service and to avoid being bumped from the queue in which trading orders were executed.

- During the late 1980s, the profit focus of brokerage houses changed drastically. Instead of investing on behalf of their clients, which for generations had been the traditional work of brokers, they were trading more and more for their own accounts, creating potential conflicts of interest. Brokers had become principals in the market, not just agents, a dangerous bypass around the Glass-Steagall Act passed by Congress in 1933 in an effort to cure financial abuses.

- Capital markets dealing in stocks, futures, options and indexes failed to synchronize. Price behavior in one market often influenced prices in other markets and created a drifting effect, "leading to near disintegration of market pricing," the Presidential Task Force concluded. At other times during the crash, the futures and stock markets were disconnected.

- "Institutional and regulatory structures designed for separate market places were incapable of dealing with a precipitate intermarket decline which brought the financial system to a brink" (the Presidential Task Force).

- Clearer than ever before, the 1987 crash demonstrated the powerful effects that markets in one country play on the markets of nearly every other nation. But no system exists to control, coordinate or regulate the complicated network of international finance trading. Despite being highly interconnected, markets in various nations operate under a myriad of rules that set different standards for such corporate practices as capitalization, accounting procedures, disclosure requirements and inside-trading. What is legal in Tokyo or Paris might send one to prison in New York.

- The 1987 crisis came as a complete surprise to the financial trading system. No contingency plan existed to cope with such gargantuan events. No single supervisory agency existed to control the several highly-integrated financial markets in the United States. No guidelines had been drawn for even minimal coordination between the different regulatory agencies that supervise U.S. markets. The financial world tried to handle the crash on a strictly unstructured ad hoc basis.

- After the crash, another dangerous speculative bubble attracted financial institutions that are supposed to avoid risks. They became deeply involved in high-risk takeovers, LBOs and junk bond transactions.

- The problems listed above caused a loss of trust and confidence in the financial market system. As the Presidential Task Force put it: "Investors began to question the value of equity assets (stocks)." This negative view of the stock market continued long after the crash and remained clearly evident when this book was written.

The financial trading system that has been followed for half a century was not designed for the extreme conditions of the late 1980s. A new model is demanded. It must meet the challenges produced by new developments in financial markets and the key role they now play in national economies around the world.

The lesson of the 1987 crash is clear: A system that is not prepared for the worst is bound to fail.

Much study, thought and planning—and courageous, farsighted leadership—will be required to solve the problems that stalk financial systems throughout the world before it is too late. But so little was being done after the crash. Does history repeat itself? In 1929, the initial crash was not enough to inspire leaders at that time to make necessary changes. The warning was ignored. It took the Great Depression of the 1930s with all its pains and sufferings to create the public reaction that, in turn, generated legislation to regulate the banking and financial industries. A functioning financial mechanism then came into being, and it worked well for a number of years. But that was more than 50 years ago.

The message of the 1987 crash comes through loud and clear:

The system no longer works.

Crafted in the early years of Franklin D. Roosevelt's administration, the old financial container that is still being used simply will not hold the many new substances that are brewing in ever more complex and interlinking world economies.

Today, the world's financial markets are ticking like a time bomb.

Appendix

The charts are taken from "Report of the Presidential Task Force on Market Mechanisms" (U.S. Government Printing Office, Washington, D.C., 1988).

FIGURE 1   The Crash Around the World

AMSTERDAM
ANP/CBS GENERAL INDEX - PRICE INDEX
From January 1, 1982 to November 12, 1987 (Weekly)

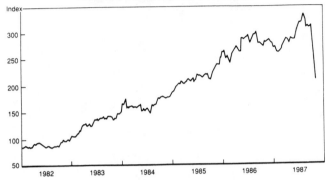

AUSTRALIA
JOINT ALL ORDINARY - PRICE INDEX
From January 1, 1982 to November 12, 1987 (Weekly)

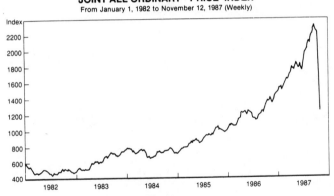

BRUSSELS
SE GENERAL - PRICE INDEX
From January 1, 1982 to November 12, 1987 (Weekly)

FIGURE 1   The Crash Around the World (continued)

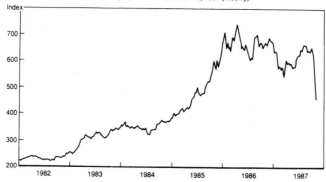

FRANKFURT
FAZ GENERAL - PRICE INDEX
From January 1, 1982 to November 12, 1987 (Weekly)

HONG KONG
HANG SENG BANK - PRICE INDEX
From January 1, 1982 to November 12, 1987 (Weekly)

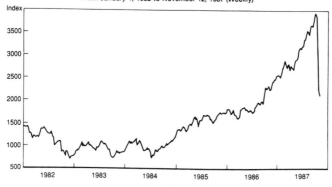

LONDON
F.T.A. ALL SHARE - PRICE INDEX
From January 1, 1982 to November 12, 1987 (Weekly)

FIGURE 1   The Crash Around the World (continued)

NEW YORK
S&P COMPOSITE - PRICE INDEX
From January 1, 1982 to November 12, 1987 (Weekly)

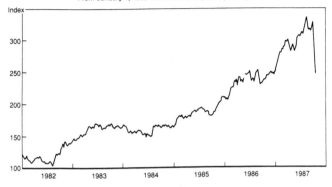

PARIS
CAC GENERAL - PRICE INDEX
From January 1, 1982 to November 12, 1987 (Weekly)

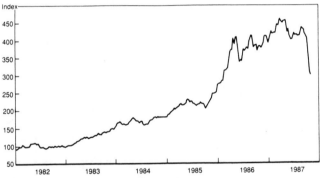

SINGAPORE
STRAITS T. INDUSTRIAL - PRICE INDEX
From January 1, 1982 to November 12, 1987 (Weekly)

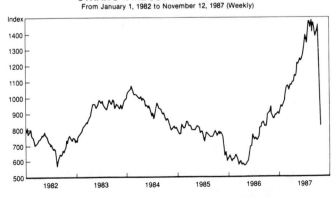

FIGURE 1   The Crash Around the World (concluded)

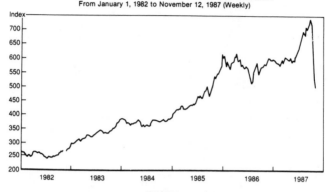

SWITZERLAND
SWISS BK CORP. INDUSTRIALS - PRICE INDEX
From January 1, 1982 to November 12, 1987 (Weekly)

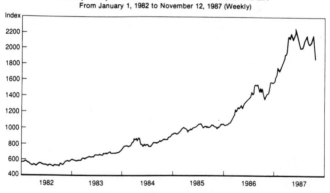

TOKYO
S.E. (NEW) ORDINARY SHARE - PRICE INDEX
From January 1, 1982 to November 12, 1987 (Weekly)

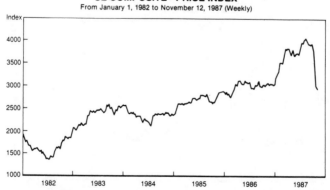

TORONTO
SE COMPOSITE - PRICE INDEX
From January 1, 1982 to November 12, 1987 (Weekly)

FIGURE 2 The U. S. Market: The Boom and the Crash

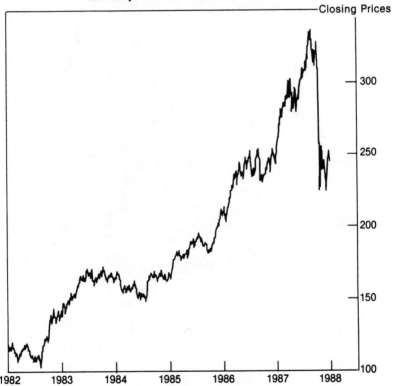

STANDARD & POOR'S 500 INDEX
January 1982 to November 1987

FIGURE 3   The U. S. Market 1986–1987

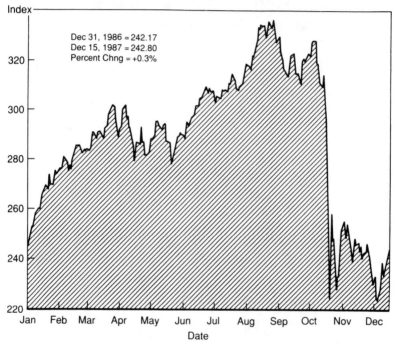

STANDARD & POOR'S 500 INDEX
Performance from Dec 31, 1986 to Dec 15, 1987

Dec 31, 1986 = 242.17
Dec 15, 1987 = 242.80
Percent Chng = +0.3%

FIGURE 4   The Crisis Minute by Minute

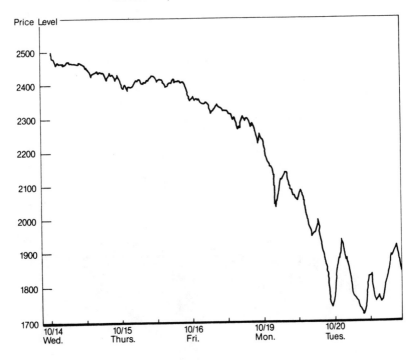

DOW JONES INDUSTRIAL ONE MINUTE CHART
October 14, 1987 to October 20, 1987

FIGURE 5   Wednesday 10/14/87

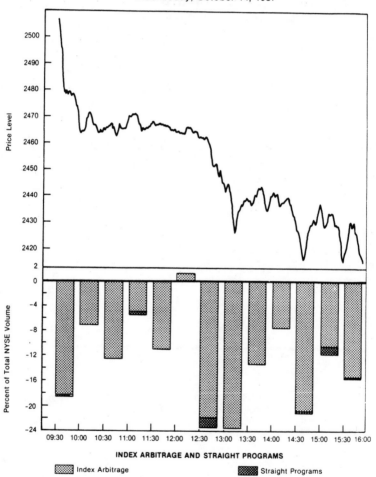

DOW JONES INDUSTRIAL ONE MINUTE CHART
Wednesday, October 14, 1987

INDEX ARBITRAGE AND STRAIGHT PROGRAMS

Index Arbitrage   Straight Programs

FIGURE 6   Thursday 10/15/87

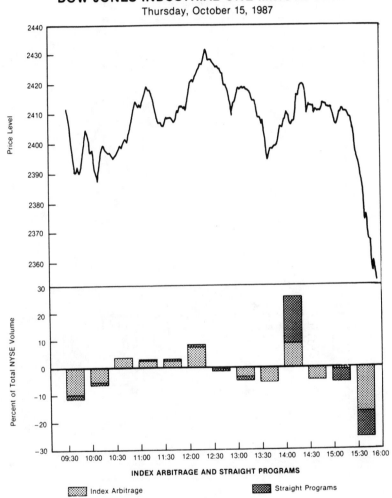

DOW JONES INDUSTRIAL ONE MINUTE CHART
Thursday, October 15, 1987

FIGURE 7   Friday 10/16/87

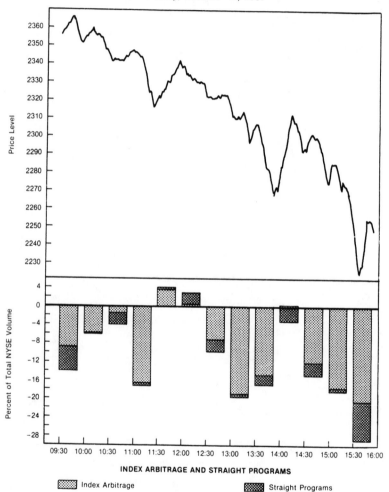

DOW JONES INDUSTRIAL ONE MINUTE CHART
Friday, October 16, 1987

FIGURE 8   Black Monday 10/19/87

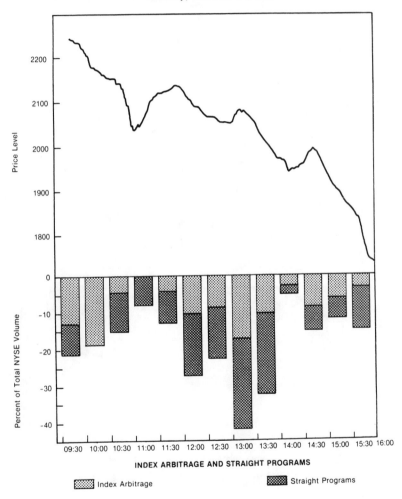

DOW JONES INDUSTRIAL ONE MINUTE CHART
Monday, October 19, 1987

FIGURE 9   Tuesday 10/20/87

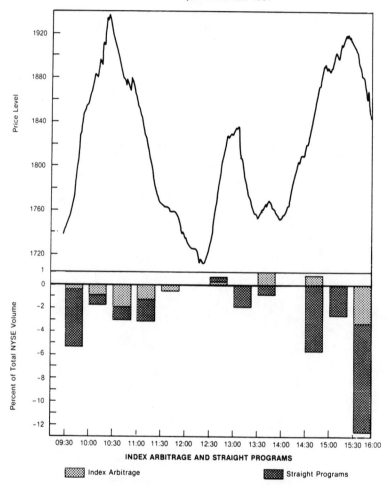

DOW JONES INDUSTRIAL ONE MINUTE CHART
Tuesday, October 20. 1987

FIGURE 10 Share Volume by Size of Transactions, Black Monday 10/19/87

SHARE VOLUME FOR ALL NYSE STOCKS

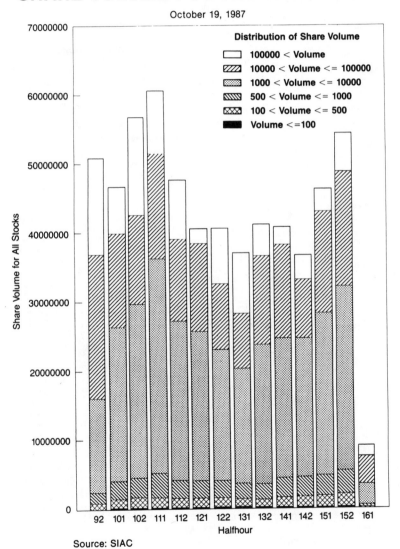

October 19, 1987

Source: SIAC

FIGURE 11   Share Volume by Size of Transactions, Tuesday 10/20/87

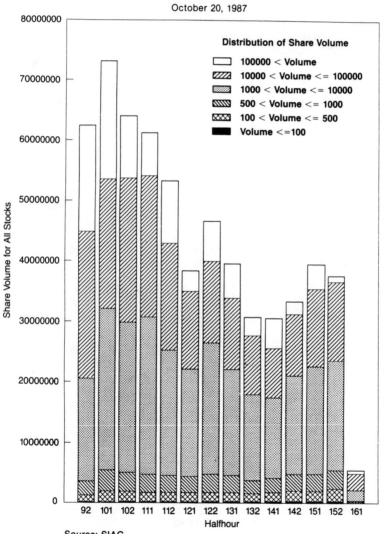

SHARE VOLUME FOR ALL NYSE STOCKS

October 20, 1987

Distribution of Share Volume

- 100000 < Volume
- 10000 < Volume <= 100000
- 1000 < Volume <= 10000
- 500 < Volume <= 1000
- 100 < Volume <= 500
- Volume <=100

Source: SIAC

FIGURE 12   Survey of Factors That Caused the Crash

The Presidential Task Force distributed questionnaires to market participants after the crash. The next three charts analyze some of the key responses.

Among fundamental factors, respondents cited three as being most significant: rising interest rates, twin deficits, and the over-valued bull market.

FUNDAMENTAL FACTORS MOST OFTEN CITED AS CAUSE OF STOCK MARKET DECLINE DURING THE WEEK PRECEDING OCTOBER 19, 1987

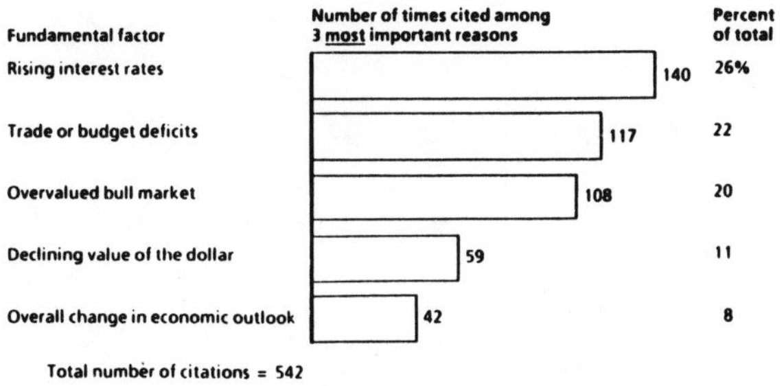

Fundamental factor	Number of times cited among 3 most important reasons	Percent of total
Rising interest rates	140	26%
Trade or budget deficits	117	22
Overvalued bull market	108	20
Declining value of the dollar	59	11
Overall change in economic outlook	42	8

Total number of citations = 542

Source General survey

On October 19, technical and psychological factors were perceived by respondents to be the most significant causes.

PERCEIVED IMPORTANCE OF FACTORS AFFECTING STOCK MARKET DECLINE ON OCTOBER 19, 1987

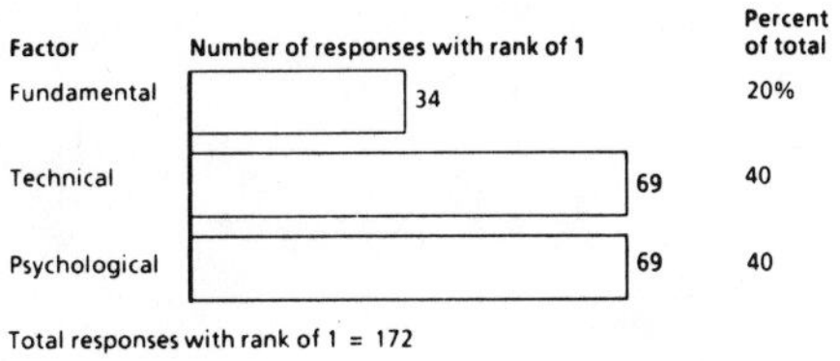

Factor	Number of responses with rank of 1	Percent of total
Fundamental	34	20%
Technical	69	40
Psychological	69	40

Total responses with rank of 1 = 172

Note: This chart is a tabulation of total responses with a rank of 1 (most important factor)

Source: General survey

FIGURE 12   Survey of Factors That Caused the Crash (concluded)

Among psychological factors cited as causes of the October 19 market decline, "panic" was the dominant cause cited, followed by "an erosion of confidence in U.S. policies" and "general nervousness in markets."

PSYCHOLOGICAL FACTORS MOST OFTEN CITED AS CAUSE OF STOCK MARKET DECLINE ON OCTOBER 19, 1987

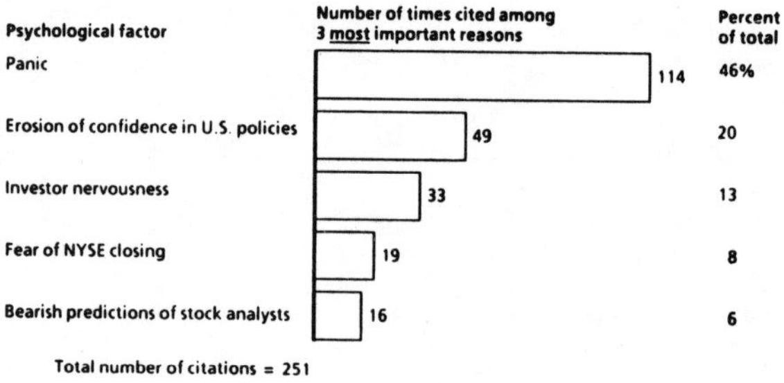

Psychological factor	Number of times cited among 3 most important reasons	Percent of total
Panic	114	46%
Erosion of confidence in U.S. policies	49	20
Investor nervousness	33	13
Fear of NYSE closing	19	8
Bearish predictions of stock analysts	16	6

Total number of citations = 251

Source: General survey

FIGURE 13   Specialist Performance

NYSE SPECIALIST PERFORMANCE [1]

	Generally counterbalanced market trends	Generally reinforced market trends	Took limited net positions
October 19..............................	58% (18)	26% (8)	16% (5)
October 20..............................	39% (12)	39% (12)	22% (7)

[1] Based on a sample of 31 NYSE stocks. Figures in parentheses represent the number of stocks from the sample in each category.

—NET DOLLAR PURCHASES OF STOCK BY NYSE SPECIALISTS (DAILY)

Date	Daily change DJIA (percent)	Net purchases [1] (millions)	TTV [2] (percent)	Specialist buying power [3] (millions)
October 14...	(3.8)	$142.8	N/A	$2,329
October 15...	(2.4)	58.5	12.5	N/A
October 16...	(4.6)	85.4	13.3	2,308
October 19...	(22.6)	485.6	17.5	852
October 20...	5.9	(457.5)	18.1	1,248

[1] A negative figure denotes net sales for the day.
[2] TTV figures are total specialist purchases plus sales of shares divided by twice the daily share volume.
[3] While the net purchase figures were calculated from audit trail data, these data are taken from NYSE capital check reports and are, therefore, not fully comparable (see discussion of source in text below). Also, these figures reflect end of day buying power.

—SPECIALIST BEHAVIOR IN 50 LARGE CAPITALIZATION STOCKS [1]

Date	Aggregate—		Fraction of specialists—	
	Final holding [2] (thousand shares)	Daily net purchases (thousand shares)	With short positions [2] (percent)	Having net sales (percent)
October 13...	429	(203)	32	58
October 14...	992	563	10	30
October 15...	1,351	359	2	38
October 16...	1,466	115	12	48
October 19...	3,694	2,228	10	30
October 20...	119	(3,575)	36	82

[1] The source for this table is NYSE opening position data.
[2] Close of business.

FIGURE 13   Specialist Performance (concluded)

—PATTERNS OF HOURLY STOCK PURCHASES AND SALES FOR 31 SPECIALISTS

[In thousands of shares]

Time	October 19				October 20			
	Shares purchased	Shares sold	Total volume	Net purchases	Shares purchased	Shares sold	Total volume	Net purchases
9:30 to 10:00	1,377	259	1,636	1,118	313	1,049	1,362	(736)
10:00 to 10:30	636	294	930	342	1,058	1,833	2,891	(775)
10:30 to 11:00	1,278	1,123	2,401	155	1,408	678	2,086	730
11:00 to 11:30	678	1,616	2,294	(938)	1,071	896	1,967	175
11:30 to 12:00	676	818	1,494	(142)	823	416	1,239	407
12:00 to 12:30	912	753	1,665	159	616	654	1,270	(38)
12:30 to 1:00	524	470	994	54	615	1,207	1,822	(592)
1:00 to 1:30	601	868	1,469	(267)	773	636	1,409	137
1:30 to 2:00	547	425	972	123	643	753	1,396	(110)
2:00 to 2:30	470	615	1,085	(145)	347	574	921	(227)
2:30 to 3:00	433	572	1,005	(139)	618	658	1,276	(40)
3:00 to 3:30	551	266	817	285	694	708	1,402	(14)
3:30 to 4:00	1,383	842	2,225	541	1,070	910	1,980	160
Total	10,066	8,921	18,987	1,146	10,049	10,972	21,021	(923)

	Specialist net liquid assets [1] (in millions)	Net liquid assets to market value [2] (percent)	Net liquid assets to trading volume [3] (percent)
1977	$185	0.023	0.123
1978	199	0.024	0.100
1979	238	0.025	0.100
1980	273	0.022	0.073
1981	284	0.025	0.073
1982	390	0.030	0.080
1983	387	0.024	0.051
1984	456	0.029	0.060
1985	441	0.023	0.045
1986	553	0.025	0.040

[1] Net liquid assets at year-end, computed in accordance with NYSE rules.
[2] Defined as net liquid assets divided by market value of shares on NYSE at year-end.
[3] Defined as net liquid assets divided by dollar value of trading volume.

Index

S

Sahl, Mort, 113
Sales volume records, 104
Savings and loan associations, 168
Sawa, Hisanichi, 35
Securities and Exchange Commission
(SEC), 4, 41-42, 45, 56, 61,
69-70, 101, 132-133
chairman, 134-137
Division of Market Regulation, 70
Securities Industry Automation
Corporation (SIAC), 38
Selling, 95
Sell-side order imbalances, 106
Shanghai Stock Exchange (China),
9-10, 125
Shareholders, 3
Silverberg, Stanley, 149
Simmons, Craig, 137
Sinai, Allen, 103
Singapore stock market, 56
Smith, Roger B., 146
Specialists, 62-66, 90, 151-152
buybacks, 110
Coca-Cola, 67-68
coping with imbalances, 101-102
Eastman Kodak, 67-68
performance, 69-70
role in Crash, 68
3M, 67-68
trading, 69-72
Spilko, Bernard, 62
Sprinkel, Beryl W., 32
Standard & Poor's Index, 40, 48, 72
Stanley, Morgan, 100
Sterling Drug, 171
Stewart, James B., 108
Stock
liquidation value, 14
purchase, 3-4
specialists, 62-66
value, 4
Stock-bond yield gap, 20
Stock index
arbitrage, 99
futures, 66-67, 99-100
Stock market, 12-13
crash in 1929, 159-160

effect on economy, 86-87
volatility, 23
Stop-loss order, 79
Straits Times Index (Singapore), 56
SuperDOT, 38
Sydney stock market (Australia), 57

T

Takeovers, 14-15, 167-168, 171
preventive measures, 177-178
Takeuchi, Michio, 94-95
Tokyo Stock Exchange (Japan), 28,
35-36, 56, 94-95
Torrenzano, Richard, 37-38
Trade deficit, 20, 25-26, 30, 33, 36,
43
Trading
index arbitrage, 74
pattern, 74-75
portfolio insurance, 74-75
suspension, 75
volume, 112-113
Treasury securities, 19, 42, 89
Triangle Publications, 171
Trust, 123-124

U

United Kingdom's stock market, 12
United Press International (UPI),
169
United States' Treasury bonds, 19
Upstairs market, 63

W

Wachtel, Larry, 155
Wall Street, 2
barometer of world's economy,
157
employment, 27, 34-35
trust, 123-124
Wall Street Journal, 21-23, 31, 38,
61, 98, 100-101, 106
109, 136, 147, 166, 171
Walton, Sam M., 103-104
Wang, An, 104
White Knight, 14
Wilshire Index, 138